The Lone Jack
King of the Mount Baker Mining District

The Lone Jack: King of the Mount Baker Mining District

Second edition published by Chuckanut Editions, Bellingham, WA.
Second edition cover and book design by Jill Flores.

Paperback ISBN: 978-1-968635-99-2
Library of Congress Number: 2025914389

Originally published by Michael G. Impero, Bellingham, Washington in 2007
Original cover and book design by Chris Rousseau.

Other titles by Michael G. Impero include:
The Lone Jack: King of the Mount Baker Mining District (2007)
Dreams of Gold (2010)
The Boys of Glacier (2013)
The Grand Lady of Mount Baker (2015)
Camp Glacier F-12: A History of the CCC Camp Glacier from 1933-1941 (2019)
Bellingham Bay and British Columbia Railroad (2020)
Towns of the North Fork Nooksack River- Vol. 1: Kendall & Maple Falls (2023)
Towns of the North Fork Nooksack River- Vol. 2: Glacier & Shuksan (2023)

The small icon of the old-time prospector used within the book is a photo of a sculpture entitled "Prospector" created by Robert Broshears of Bremerton.
Cover photo: Headwork construction—upper tramway. (WWU-CPNWS)
Page 1: Roy Gargett (J. Munroe)
Back cover photo: Bear Mountain (J. Munroe)

Printed in the United States of America.

Chuckanut Editions
1200 11th Street
Bellingham, WA 98225
villagebooks.com
publishing@villagebooks.com

Other titles in the Chuckanut Editions catalogue include:
Shipyard: Short Histories of Whatcom County's Boatbuilders & Shipyards
Geology of the San Juan Islands
The Colophon Café Cookbook
Fairhaven: A History

CHUCKANUT
EDITIONS

This book is dedicated to:

Frances Bruce Todd who was the first true historian of the Upper Nooksack River Valley "The Trail through the Woods" and who gave encouragement to the author to write about the Mt. Baker Gold Rush and the Lone Jack.

Jake Steiner, the resident historian of Glacier and the upper Nooksack River, opened his home and memory to the author every time information was needed.

Susie Impero, my partner and wife of 46 years.

To all of those who helped:

Thanks
Tom Anderson
Bellingham Library
Tom Brown
Dave Brumbaugh
John Christenson
Elaine Dick
René Dove
Jason Gaber
Steve Gaber
Rolland Holterman
Andrene Knapp
Robert Krammer
Charlotte Kvistad
Russ Lambert
Steve Lohse
Shirley Post-Plummer
Chris Secrist
U.S. Forest Service
University of Washington
Wa. State Dept. of Natural Resources
Western Washington University Archives
Western Washington University CPNS
Whatcom Museum

Special Thanks
John Bullene
Gerrit Byeman
John Munroe
Chris Rousseau
Jake Steiner
Chuck Stone

Table of Contents

Chapter 1
Discovery
1

Chapter 2
Partners
9

Chapter 3
Gold Rush
19

Chapter 4
Early Development
36

Chapter 5
Lone Jack Gold
58

Chapter 6
Brooks-Willis
93

Chapter 7
Later Years
128

Chapter 8
Last Sourdough
139

Chapter 9
Jack's Ghosts
171

Index 174

Map 1
Anderson's Map of Mount Baker or Nooksack Mining District 178

Map 2
General Layout of Surface Development at Lone Jack 180

Map 3
Lone Jack Workings 1898 – 1907 181

Chapter 1
Discovery

August 23, 1897 started differently than the six days before it. The dense clouds and rain that had hung over the Cascade Mountains for almost a week suddenly cleared and the sun shone brightly on the wonderland around Twin Lakes. Jack Post, an old sourdough who had prospected in the area for over 10 years, woke at dawn. He started coffee for himself and his two prospecting partners—Russ Lambert, a lawyer, and Luman Van Valkenburg, a logger. All three of them were from Sumas. The three had been camped at Twin Lakes for over two weeks prospecting as much of the surrounding area as possible. At an elevation of 5,200 feet, this August morning was as cold as any clear morning at Twin Lakes; a blanket of frost covered the camp and a light layer of ice formed on the lake edge. Post and his companions had needed the weather to improve to complete the high area searching.

Regardless of the sudden break in weather, their food supplies had run low, forcing them to head back to Sumas early. Luckily for them, however, an old prospector acquaintance of Post named Jack Treutle wandered into their camp on his own return to Sumas. Upon hearing their predicament, Treutle offered Post all the spare food he had.

East Twin Lake, elevation 5,200 feet. (M. Impero)

After eating a sparse breakfast, the three decided that Post would head out to the high area on the east side of Bear Mountain. Russ Lambert would head to a high route on the west side of Red Mountain and Lyman Van Valkenburg would travel high on the east side of Red Mountain. Post and Lambert had named all the mountains, lakes, and passes in the area on previous trips. A few days before, they had discovered a small amount of color in the West Fork of Silesia Creek and in the headwaters of Swamp Creek. They all left camp that day determined to locate the source.

Post headed from the campsite through Twin Lakes Pass to the east. He passed a third small lake that he had named Winchester Lake along with the mountain, Winchester Mountain. This area is alpine and mostly above timberline. From there, he held his elevation and headed in a southerly direction, finally stopping on a ridge extending down off Bear Mountain.

Post looked across what was later named Whist Creek and spotted a large outcropping of quartz running diagonally up the mountain face and over the next ridge. Pursuing it, he started down to the creek bottom and then ascended straight up to the vein. He climbed a series of small cliffs to reach the quartz. Post broke off a piece and determined with a quick look that it had potential.

Bear Mountain and Lulu Gulch. (M. Impero)

Bear Mountain from across Silesia Creek, 1940 (U of W)
Point A: Location of the Discovery Lone Jack vein, 1897
Point B: Top of aerial tram at Lone Jack portal
Point C: Bottom of tram at Mt. Baker Mining Co. stamp mill and camp
Point D: Lulu portal
Point E: Brooks-Willis mill site & camp
Point F: Lulu Gulch
Point G: Garrison Creek drainage
Point H: U.S. land monument No. 1

Post followed the vein up and beyond the ridge, then dropped down under a group of 300-foot cliffs. He proceeded to the south, gaining elevation, and eventually rose above the cliffs and spotted the vein again. As Post climbed nearer, the terrain became extremely steep. A lesser-experienced prospector may have had a major problem with this terrain, but with all his years in these mountains, Post maneuvered easily in this difficult area.

Finally he arrived at the vein. Using his constant friend, a rock hammer, Post started to work on the quartz. The rock appeared extremely rich and, upon looking closely, he could see gold flecks suspended in the quartz. It was the shock of his life. Post almost fell off the small ledge with excitement.

Surface quartz vein 16 to 18 inches wide. (S. Gaber)

Quartz vein on Bear Mountain. (M. Impero)

Steep east side of Bear Mountain. (M. Impero)

First opening of Lone Jack operation (M. Impero)

4

Post spent a period of time seeking any signs that an earlier prospecting party had made the discovery, but found none. He then loaded his pack with some chosen samples and headed back toward camp. While excited, he moved slowly, aware that at any point he could be in an extremely unsafe position.

The first man back to camp had the task of building the fire, putting on the coffee and opening the last two cans of beans. Van Valkenburg returned first that day and a few minutes later Lambert also came into view. The two discussed their day. Both had found traces of color but nothing different than that of the past days. Then, standing around their campfire, they heard shouting from across the east lake: "Found the son of a bitch! Found the son of a bitch!" They looked through the nighttime haze and saw Post half-running and half-walking toward them, an ear-to-ear smile across his face. As soon as Post arrived he relived his day and showed the samples. Afterward, a snort out of the old jug was more than required, and the men discussed the find into the late hours of the night, surely finishing the contents of the bottle.

The group decided that one of them should return to Sumas for the needed assay report. If the ore was determined to be of the expected high grade, that person would then travel to Whatcom, the county seat, to file the claims. After a drawing of straws, Lambert, the lawyer, was chosen to go. The selection of Lambert turned out to be a bit of luck, as Lambert's representation would provide them needed legal support in the future.

John Bullene returning toward Twin Lakes. (M. Impero)

Typical claim marker. (M. Impero)

No. 43013 John Post   No 1   (copy)   Notice of Location   Lone Jack
Notice is hereby given that the undersigned, having complied
with the requirements of chapter six of title thirty two of the Revised
statutes of the United States, and the local customs, laws and regulations, has located 1500 linear feet on the Lone Jack lode, situated
in unorganized Mining District, Whatcom County, Washington.
and described as follows to wit: Beginning at discovery stake where
this notice is posted and running along the lode in a northerly
direction 1500 ft. With Surface ground 300. wide on each side of
center line. The boundaries being marked by stone monuments
3 ft high (containing marked stake.) at each of the corners and at
northerly center end. This claim is about 3½ miles in a northerly
direction from 19 mi. post on Ruby Creek trail and on the east slope
of Bear mountain between Silesia creek and Swamp creek. and is bounded
on the northerly end by Sidney claim and on the southerly end
by Jennie claim.
Discovered Aug 23rd 1897
Located Aug. 23rd 1897   John Post Locator.
Witnesses
   R. S. Lambert
   L. G. Van Valkenburg
           Received for record at 10 am Sept 4 A. D. 1897, and recorded at the request of
           R.S. Lambert   ALEX. VAN WYCK, County Auditor of Whatcom County, State of W

Lone Jack claim filing. (Washington State Archives)

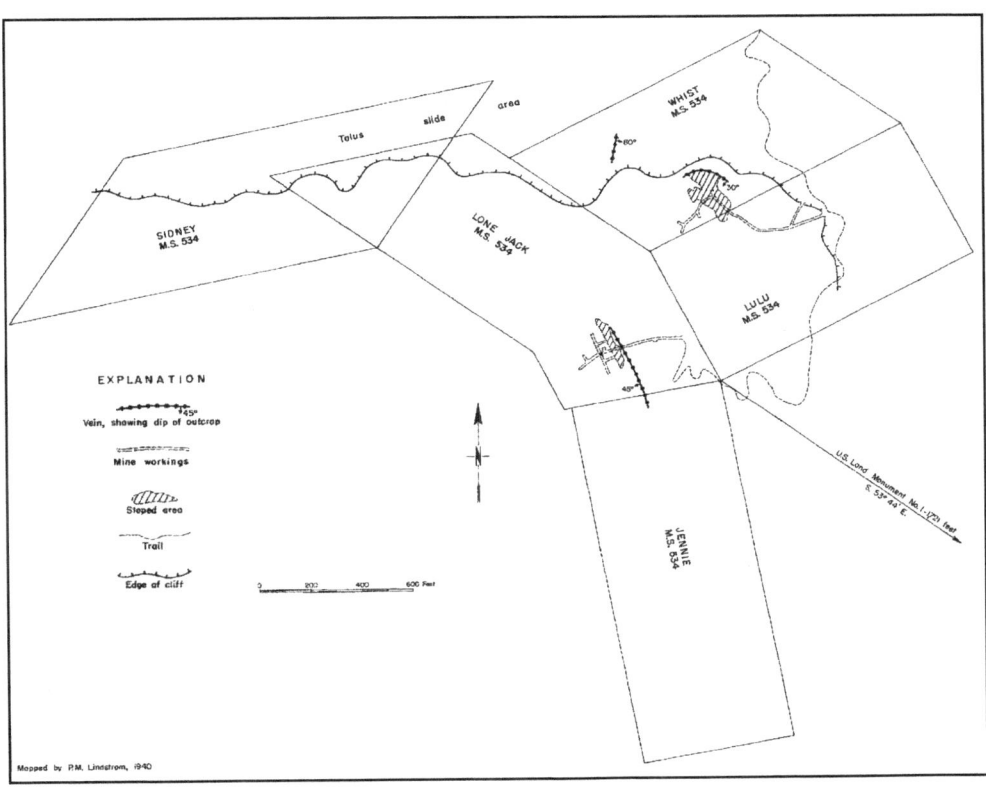

Layout of Post-Lambert claims. (C. Stone)

For several days, the men worked at top speed, stripping rock high on the mountainside where the gold-bearing ore was discovered, blazing witness trees, and staking and stepping off the claims. In the north area, where the terrain was too steep to stake, they marked a corner by throwing over a cliff an empty tobacco can with a note folded neatly inside. When the staking and posting of the claims was completed, Lambert headed back to Sumas.

In reviewing the document and map above, one finds no surveying reference points because the find is in the wilderness and reference points for the area weren't known at the time. Another noteworthy mention is that the recorder in the county office wrote "Ruby Creek," not "Ruth Creek." This error is likely because the recorder was so accustomed to writing "Ruby Creek" on all of the claims he had recorded earlier from the Slate Creek Mining District. The Lone Jack Claim was documented on pages immediately following claims Post and Van Valkenburg had filed for other areas.

John Knuehmann, a tailor in Sumas, was the recognized assayer in the area. On August 31, 1897, Knuehmann's family house sat on rollers in the middle of Main Street as he moved it to a location in town. After Lambert met with him and showed him the samples of ore for the assay,

Knuehmann determined the samples to be extremely high grade, valuing them at $3,585 per ton.

Lambert, upon getting the expected information, headed directly to Whatcom to file the claims in the Auditor's Office. There, he filed five claims: Discovery No. 1, "Lone Jack," for Post; Claim No. 2, "Jenny," for Van Valkenburg; and No. 3, "Sidney," for himself. The remaining two claims, the "Lulu" and the "Whist," Lambert named jointly for all three. Knuehmann, after completing his report, lost all interest in his house-moving project. He packed up his prospecting gear and struck out at dawn for Twin Lakes. His family home was left in the middle of the roadway for a few weeks with his family still in it. The Mt. Baker gold rush had begun.

Assayer crucible. (M. Impero)

Assayer's gold scale. (M. Impero)

Lone Jack Corporation 7795 Zell Road Custer, Washington U.S.A. 98240 Attention: Mr. Tom Anderson							

Ⅼⓐⓑ ⓉⒺⓈⓉ ltd.
1650 PANDORA STREET, VANCOUVER, B.C., V5L 1L6

Telex 04 54210

Certificate of Assay

File No. 7818 D

Date   September 23, 1980

We hereby Certify that the following are the results of assays made by us upon submitted ...... Ore ...... samples.

Sample Identification	GOLD Ounces Per Ton	SILVER Ounces Per Ton	Percent	Percent	Percent	Percent	Percent	Percent
A	0.006	0.01						
B	0.090	11.07						
C	1.53	0.58						
D	0.005	L 0.01						
E	3.42	0.84						
F	0.006	L 0.01						
X-1	0.120	0.08						
L = Less Than								

Sample of an assayer report. (T. Anderson)

Chapter 2

Partners

The three partners of the Post-Lambert/Lone Jack Discovery were the most mismatched collection of men that one could imagine. There was Jack Post, the free-spirited mountain-man, whose life-long ambition was to be a successful prospector and to which end he spent all of his obtainable time and resources. Russ S. Lambert, the educated and professional lawyer, also had the lifelong desire to make his living as a prospector, and took each opportunity he found to escape from his profession and head out with Post or others. Luman Van Valkenburg, a logger and land clearer, had a love for prospecting but his desires were more as a hobbyist. These three had been a prospecting partnership off and on for a matter of five years.

Jack Post

John (Jack) Post was born in an old western fort near Josephine County, Oregon, in 1860. At age 9, his parents moved to Curry County, Oregon, and there he received his formal education.

L.G. Van Valkenburg and Jack Post (right) about to leave Sumas on a prospecting trip to the mountains. (J. Munroe)

In 1880, Jack struck out for himself and, for several years, engaged in mining and prospecting near Yreka, Calif. After moving to Washington in 1886, Jack used Seattle as his headquarters while making his living at prospecting, hunting, and trapping.

In 1887 he journeyed north to Whatcom County. On this first visit, he passed through Sumas and continued through the Canadian border, where he prospected with thousands of others at the Boston Bar Strike on the Fraser River. Following a period of no success, with provisions running low and no available grubstake, he reappeared in Sumas, where he settled down.

After a few years of searching the district, Jack declared openly to the surprise of all the old sourdoughs living in the Sumas area that there would be a major gold strike discovered in the local mountains. With this in mind, he devoted his entire effort to his cause.

Following his arrival in Sumas, the town folks found him to be a man of unusual physical stamina, resourcefulness and courage. In 1889, he married Lillian Eaton, daughter of the first blacksmith in Sumas. In the late 1880's, Post built a new residence on Cherry Street in Sumas, using the proceeds from the sale of a mining claim.

When mining income was slow and there was a need for a more stable paycheck, Post would occasionally be employed for the B.B. & B.C. Railroad in Sumas. He became a close friend of Jack Treutle, the engineer who ran B.B. & B.C. Engine No. 3 into Sumas. Treutle later died in his cab as his engine ran away on a steep grade near Acme. In memoriam, Jack and Lillian Post named their youngest son Treutle.

Post operated in and out of several business deals around town and for a time he was partner in the Bodega Saloon. This made the Bodega his favorite hangout, although he never actually worked there. Post made money as an unlicensed, part-time real-estate dealer out of the Bodega as he had an idea for where homestead rights had been relinquished. If a newcomer wanted to get a location on an available piece of ground, they simply located Post with a fair proposition ready.

Jack Post at the time of the discovery. (J. Munroe)

Jack Post on a later prospecting trip.
(S. Post-Plummer)

With his real-estate savvy, among other good runs of luck, Post could be a moneymaker; however, only a few times in his life did the good luck continue for any period of time. His normal way of life was working from one grubstake to another, and it made little difference to him if the stakes were large or small.

After Post discovered the Lone Jack in 1897 and became famous and recognized in the region, he received a letter from the U.S. Forest Reserve. The letter offered him an appointment as a U.S. forest ranger, without salary, for the Mt. Baker District. Had he accepted this offer, he would have been the first man so appointed. The letter went on to read, "Any unusual or dangerous condition you will immediately report to your superior." At the word "superior," Post stopped reading the letter, looking to his wife Lillian and she asked immediately. "Well now, Jack, how are you going to like that?"

"I'm not going to like it, Lillian," Post replied. "A harness would soon make blisters on me." The

government, assuming that Jack would eagerly accept this position, which he did not, shipped him a complete box of assigned tools. Jack was proud of these furnished "government tools" and used them for years around the house and up in the mountains. R.S. Lambert, Post's mining partner and servant of the government in almost all causes, was appointed to this position in 1900 and he held the position until 1904.

Post's constant companion on all of his mountain excursions was his trusted Winchester 30/30 rifle. Winchester Mountain, which currently provides the location for a forest fire lookout, is situated to the north of Twin Lakes and was named by Post after that trusty 30/30. Bear Mountain, on some maps named Lone Jack Mountain, was another mountain named by Post while prospecting. Located between Winchester Mountain and Bear Mountain lie two beautiful alpine lakes, which Post named Twin Lakes.

There were two incidents in which the Winchester performed a service other than its expected needs up in the mountains. Post had a neighbor named Hogan in Sumas and it seems that Hogan's chickens were constantly crossing the imaginary border into the Post backyard and creating a mess. One day Hogan heard a commotion coming from the backyard and, assuming that someone's dog or a wild animal was pursuing his chickens, he grabbed his shotgun and went rushing out to investigate. Seeing Post, Hogan said, "Oh, it's you, Jack Post!"

"Yes, and you better keep your damn birds off my property or I'll turn the dog on them," yelled Post. Hogan slowly leveled his shotgun directly at Post and yelled back, "Better you leave my chickens alone."

Post stared for a moment at the muzzle of the threatening shotgun with his dark eyes, looked Hogan squarely in the eye and shouted, "Oh. So that's the way you want to play, is it? Just wait here a minute and we'll see!"

Post turned and dashed to his house, quickly mounted the three steps and almost immediately reappeared with his Winchester. He deftly slipped a few cartridges into the magazine, levered one cartridge into the barrel, and then started across his backyard in the direction of Hogan standing near a corner fence. As Hogan saw Post approaching, he quickly decided that he wanted no part of Post's manner, headed across his yard and returned into his house. Later on, Hogan butchered his chickens and brought an end to the famous Sumas Chicken Manure Disagreement.

The other incident involved a manhunt for a man who was a known sheep thief. Post, with the help of his cougar hound, was part of the posse. In the process of following the thief across the border and catching him, the thief shot and killed Post's hound.

That night after the thief had been placed in the Sumas Jail by the marshal, Post went around back in the darkness with the rifle across his arm. Upon finding the right window

with the thief inside, Post said through the opening, "Hey, there fellow, I hear you're the one that shot my dog. When you get out of here I'm going to shoot you." The thief didn't like the promise in the tone and realized that Jack meant business. He managed to pry the bars apart, and later that night he escaped, not to be seen again in Whatcom County.

Jack Post with his wife Lillian had a family of five children: three girls and two boys. Jack also filled the position of town marshal and constable of Sumas. Mrs. Post's occupation was listed in the Sumas census report as a "wash woman and caretaker of the elderly."

Post was a man who, when he had money, spent it. After the sale of the Lone Jack in 1897, Post became a wealthy man overnight and there are various stories of his spending. Following the sale, he traveled to the Fairhaven Hotel in Fairhaven, the most luxurious hotel in the county, and rented the most elaborate suite for a week. There, he enjoyed life as high as possible, buying expensive food and drinks for all.

By 1906, Clifford Post, Jack's oldest son, had spent a great amount of his early years in the mountains prospecting and hunting with his father. In that year Jack and Clifford purchased a 16-foot boat in Lynden, loaded their gear, and paddled down the Nooksack River to salt-water. Then went up the coast past Vancouver to Squamish. There, they began hand-logging along the steep sides of the inlet, and when they made enough money for a grubstake, they would head off into the mountains again. In this manner the two worked their way north and, after acquiring a larger boat, made it all the way to Alaska in 1909.

Once the father-son team eventually returned to Sumas, Jack Post set to prospecting again but this time on the north side of the border. He worked an area north of the Chilliwack River and staked numerous claims in the region. This time, however, the Canadian government required two months of assessment work per year on each claim for the claimant to hold his rights. This limited the number of claims someone could lay stake to.

Post became a friend with a German man by the name of Hipkope, who lived with his wife and a family of eight daughters and two sons up the Chilliwack River, where they operated a boarding house. The boarding house was utilized as an overnight point for miners using both sides of the border. Hipkope, a national German, was disliked by his neighbors and often accused of being a spy for the German government. Following an investigation by the Canadian government, Hipkope was placed in a Canadian prison camp, leaving his wife and family alone up in the wilderness.

Post spent a large amount of his spare time checking in on the girls, concerned about their well-being and safety—especially with all those miners present in the area. Jack, in performing the safeguarding duties, still managed to allow one of the girls to marry a miner, though that miner was Jack's son Clifford. Clifford's wife died at a young age and he remained a miner/beekeeper the rest of his life.

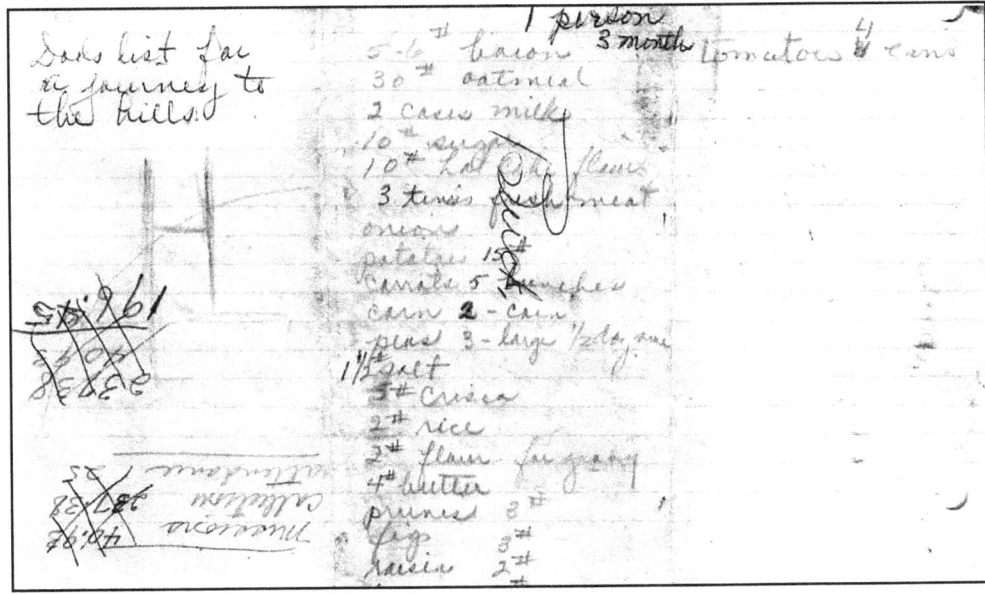

Jack Post's grocery list. (S. Post-Plummer)

Jack and Clifford Post. (S. Post-Plummer)

Every two to three weeks Jack Post, year round, would say, "I hear the hills calling and it's time for me to go."

In later life and with the years catching up with him, Post took a position as caretaker for a family that owned Blakely Island in the San Juan Islands. As a recluse, he lived alone down near the beach in a small cabin he built.

At this time, a sawmill operated on the north end of the island near where Post lived and he salvaged all the lumber he could from the mill. Post built a small flatbottom boat from the salvaged lumber and on which he and his dog paddled around among the islands. One of his granddaughters named Shirley lived on Lopez Island and he traveled to see her on calm days. After a few years, with health problems catching up with him, Post moved to live with his sister down on the Oregon Coast.

Shortly thereafter, the cabin Post lived in caught fire and he was badly burned. He died a short time later and was buried in Oregon. Post died a very tired, worn-out man with not a penny to his name. Yet, if given the chance to re-live his life, the second time around would have probably been exactly the same. ***"If I could only see and do the things I have seen and done."***

Russ S. Lambert

There was a time when Russ Lambert, as mayor, was having difficulty obtaining a marshal for Sumas. He'd been through four volunteers during the last month but none of these could hold their position in the "only wet town in the county" and this made him determined to locate a new long-term replacement.

Lambert figured he would have to hire somebody very special to straighten things out—someone good. Lambert took a walk up Cherry Street, seeking out a tall athletic fellow that he had in mind, a man who had served well as deputy on a few occasions. He soon located Grover Crooks.

Child painting of Jack Post. (S. Post-Plummer)

"Hello, Grover," said Lambert. "I want to see you down in my office."

"What's up, Mr. Lambert?"

"Plenty, Grover. You're going to be the next chief of police in this town."

"Me? Why, I haven't been figuring that way."

"Well, now's the time you start figuring and acting. You'll have plenty of action, but I know you can do it, and I don't mind saying. I don't know another man in town I'd have more confidence in."

Crooks was surprised. He summed up the situation as they headed down Cherry Street.

"Oh, come to think of it, I can't do it, Mr. Lambert. I'm not 21 yet. You probably didn't know that."

"Not 21! That doesn't seem possible, Grover! Didn't you play ball in the Texas League even before you came to Sumas?"

"Yes, that's right, but they called me 'The Boy Wonder' and so when I came here I didn't let anyone know I was still under age. I know people think I'm well up in my 20s, but I'm still three months short of 21."

"Well, Grover that surprises me," Lambert said. "In fact, if I didn't know you as well as I do, I wouldn't be able to believe that. It would surprise anyone else in town, too, so I don't see as it makes any difference at all. Besides, you know I'm an attorney and if there are any legal angles I'll take care of them. Just you go ahead now, and don't bring up that point again."

By this time they had reached Lambert's office. Lambert opened a drawer in his roll-top desk, took out a Colt pistol, a pair of handcuffs, and pinned a badge on the mackinaw of Crooks. "Now, you're the chief of police. I want you to keep order in town. Use your own methods and remember I'm behind you all the way. The keys to the jail are on the paddle in there."

Russ Lambert at the time of the discovery. (J. Munroe)

Lambert was born Sept. 16, 1867, in Belvedere, Ill. After attending public school, he graduated in 1889 from Wesley University Law School in Bloomington. He then was admitted to the bar and practiced for a year in Illinois.

Lambert arrived in Whatcom in 1890 and in December of that year opened a law office in Sumas. The reason that Lambert traveled to Sumas was easy to follow. He discovered that Sumas, a new town being formed on the United States/Canada border, had no other attorney practicing law. His first official act was that of incorporating the City of Sumas. Russ married Carrie Swail, also of Belvedere. She traveled to Sumas where they raised a family of four children: Louise, Sidney, Esther, and John.

Lambert was unbelievably active in political matters in Sumas, Whatcom County, and Olympia. He served as the mayor of Sumas in 1895 and 1898, as the town clerk, school director, and U.S. Forest Reserve ranger from 1900 to 1904, the position that Jack Post refused to accept. Lambert was a staunch Republican and served in Olympia as a representative in 1905, 1907 and 1909, and as a state senator in 1921 and 1923. On a personal note, he was a Mason, an Elks and a member of the Odd Fellows. Russ Lambert also served as president of Garrison Brothers State Bank in Sumas.

With his time divided among family, business, government, and prospecting, he was a man who was constantly in motion. Lambert's main hobby in his free time was prospecting. Repeatedly, as soon as the snow melted, he headed back to the mountains with friends or by himself.

Russ Lambert in the House of Representatives in Olympia. (R. Lambert)

Lambert was a much-respected man on both sides of the border. However, in one incident he was not recognized. Going into the mountains to prospect and stay for a couple of months, he would return home with a full beard, having the look of a tramp. On one occasion, Lambert headed home to Sumas via a different route, through Chilliwack.

As always, carrying his gun, he stopped at a restaurant to get something to eat. It turned out there had been a train robbery in the days before. As he sat enjoying his lunch, Lambert noticed the place gradually emptied itself. Then the Northwest Mounted Police entered and he had to explain to the police who he was.

Lambert became a very somber, abrupt and gruff man as life went on. He had a handle-bar mustache, wore a large western-type hat, and a constant

Four generations of Lambert men, Russ is on the left. (R. Lambert)

cloud of cigar smoke wafted about his head. Small children, including his grandchildren, were scared of him, avoiding him if possible. His wife Carrie died in January 1911. Following her death, Lambert became a lady's man and would be seen all over town courting women.

One of his granddaughters had a job of reporting to his office after school on Tuesdays and making telephone calls for her grandfather. She called different numbers and was told if a man answered to hang up but if a woman answered to hand the phone to Grandpa. Lambert needed the little girl to help call the women because the phone operator would have recognized his voice.

Lambert named two of the original Lone Jack claims after two of his children; the Lulu named after Louise and the Sidney after Sidney. Lambert passed away in Sumas in 1944 at 77 years old.

Luman Van Valkenburg

Luman G. Van Valkenburg, born on March 3, 1862 to George and Almena Van Valkenburg in Durand, Il., was one of Sumas' earliest settlers. After arriving in the area of Sumas in 1882, Van Valkenburg homesteaded west of the later townsite location where there were only two other settlers at the time: A.R. Johnson and J.B. Perry. On this homestead, a small stream flowed toward the east and Van Valkenburg named it Van Valkenburg Creek.

Van Valkenburg hauled the lumber for the first building in Sumas. Matilda Jane Post, being no relation to Jack Post, arrived in Sumas in 1883 with the Manley Rogers family. On Feb. 15, 1887, she married Van Valkenburg. They made their first home on his homestead west of town.

After the initial work of developing the homestead the family, which now included a daughter, Josephine, moved to a mill community called Tuxedo, located on the Hill Road east of Nooksack. Van Valkenburg hauled logs out of the woods by horse and wagon for the mill while Matilda was equally busy cooking at the cookhouse. Lydia was born at Tuxedo.

Luman Van Valkenburg with his wife at about the time of discovery. (J. Munroe)

Van Valkenburg sold his homestead in 1896, relocated in town in the annex of a larger building that the family used as a lodging house. He later used the two-story building as a store, then remodeled a portion to be used as a schoolhouse.

With the move to town, he formed a friendship with Jack Post and Russ Lambert and the three began making trips to the Cascade Mountains. Soon enough, the group located the rich outcropping of the five claims they called the "Lone Jack." Van Valkenburg had stock in the Mt. Baker Mining Co. and kept this ownership until he sold out in 1918.

Van Valkenburg was actively engaged in gold mining claims, not only at Mount Baker Mining District but also in the Republic, Wash. area and in Alaska. He was also one of the original locators and later full owner of the Silver Tip Mine. After the mining fever subsided, he opened a real estate and insurance office. He served on the Sumas City Council and also as city clerk and justice of the peace.

Van Valkenburg died July 15, 1922 while working in the U.S. Forest Service shop in Glacier. He had been employed for the Forest Service for two years and he was 60 years old. One of the pallbearers serving at his funeral was his old prospecting friend Russ Lambert.

Chapter 3

Gold Rush

With the discovery of gold on Bear Mountain, the Mt. Baker Gold Rush was upon Whatcom County. The State of Washington faced economic depression in the early 1890s and the discovery created a much-needed boost for the region.

Sumas, on the U.S.-Canada border, was the closest town to the new gold district and was served at the time by several railroads, one of which—the Bellingham Bay/British Columbia Railroad (B.B. & B.C.), provided passenger service to and from Whatcom, the county seat. Whatcom saw an exodus of young men immediately following the discovery. Prospective miners hurried to stake their claims before the rest of the country showed up and also to beat the winter weather that was rapidly approaching.

Banning Austin and the Search for A Cascade Route

The first topographical maps of the mountainous area of Whatcom County became available after the United States/Canada Northwest Boundary Survey of 1857-1858. In 1893, a group headed up by a man named Banning Austin was assigned the task of locating a northern crossing of the Cascade Range, providing access to Eastern Washington, while passing through the gold fields of east Whatcom County.

The proposed route headed up the North Fork of the Nooksack River, to the mouth of Ruth Creek, then followed Ruth Creek to Hannegan Pass. The Banning Austin Party believed that in reaching Hannegan Pass (about 5,400 feet high) the summit of the Cascade Mountains had been reached, which later proved to be false. When Austin discovered Hannegan Pass, his group also discovered a second pass over the divide linking Mt. Baker and Mt. Shuksan, which he named Wild Goose Pass. This pass was later renamed Austin Pass. With the discovery of this second pass, a member of the Austin Party inscribed on a tree trunk in the pass, a record which remains today.

Representation of inscription. (C. Rousseau)

Following the review of the proposed route, the state Legislature stepped in with the passage of "an act to provide for the establishment of a state road through the Cascade Mountains via a pass north of Mt. Baker, to connect eastern and western Washington, and providing an appropriation therefore." The act initiated the creation of the Cascade State Road Commission with the appointment of T.P. Hannegan as chairman in 1893. Hannegan was then succeeded by John Cryderman as chairman with J.J. Donovan and F.G. Oliver as members of the board.

An appropriation of $20,000 was set aside with the condition that Whatcom County appropriate an additional $6,000 and Okanogan and Stevens counties each appropriate $1,000. The funds were to be placed in the state trust for use by the forenamed commissioners. The starting point of the proposed road was to commence "where Glacier Creek empties into the North Fork of the Nooksack running hence by the best practical route north of Mt. Baker to a point on the Columbia River opposite the town of Marcus, Stevens County," a distance of about 200 miles.

In late 1893, the proposed Cascade State Wagon Road had been surveyed to within four miles of Hannegan Pass. Continuing work included the clearing of fallen timber and the corduroying of wet places.

Work went on through the early months of 1894. Around this time came more reliable reports of other expeditions giving evidence that building a road through the Cascades

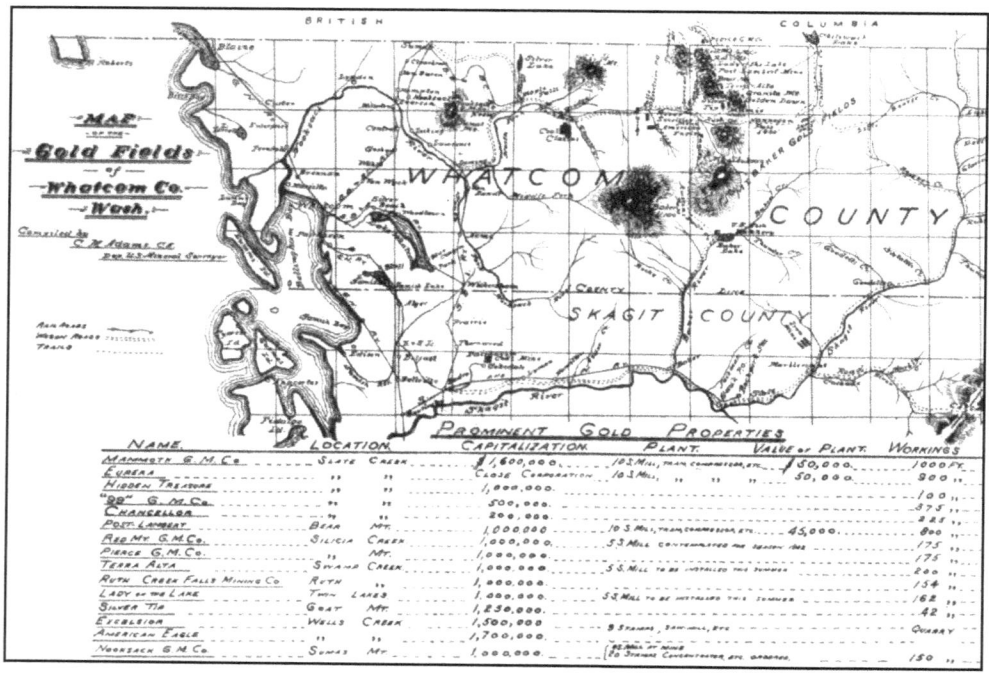

Map of gold fields in western Whatcom County (Mount Baker Mining District). (J. Munroe)

at the planned location was thoroughly impractical due to steep grades and high altitudes. What had been built so far was with a very crude trail suitable for travel when blanketed by snow and suitable for horses only in dry summer months. Work halted and the Cascade State Wagon Road thenceforth existed in name only.

All Roads Lead to Loop's Inn

In 1897, the only used route to the Post-Lambert was the U.S. Route, which involved crossing over Mamie Pass above Ruth Creek on the proposed Cascade Wagon Trail at Mile Post 19.5. The route to the gold fields began at Sumas, but began for most with a train journey to Sumas from Whatcom on the B.B. & B.C. railroad.

Following that, the 18-mile wagon road headed southeast to the foothills. The road turned up Saar Creek Canyon and continued up to Keese (later named Kendall). It continued up the valley to Hardan (later named Maple Falls), and then to the termination of the crude road at Loop's Inn, a ranch owned by Albert Loop and his wife. The B.B. & B.C. advertised that not only did it connect with sound steamers on the bay but that it also provided a passenger train each morning that connected with a stage at Sumas that then traveled daily to Loop's Inn.

Following the discovery at Lone Jack, a 29-mile alternate route opened from Whatcom to Loop's Inn, a route which would later become the Mt. Baker Highway. One report states that the first 11 miles of this new route,

from Whatcom to Nugent's Bridge was a suitable plank road and that the remaining 18 miles to Loop's was a "well traveled" gravel road. Another report states that the roadbed had no gravel on it and was impassable during the wet season.

Alfred B. Loop and his wife Martha, along with their two oldest sons, had settled on three timber claims located about one mile west of Boulder Creek in 1888. The site where their home stood is now the residence of Ruth Hansen. In total, the Loop family had seven sons and two daughters.

Loop, an old Union Civil War soldier, was the appointed postmaster for the Hardan Post Office from 1893 to 1895. With the help of her two daughters, Mrs. Loop operated a popular eating establishment (the last one up the route in 1897) and also furnished overnight facilities. During the gold rush, two of the sons, D.J. and Harry, provided pack trains to the mines around the Twin Lakes area. At that time, before the bridges were constructed, the miners and packers had to ford the treacherous North Fork of the Nooksack River twice and Glacier Creek once going each direction.

With the Mt. Baker Gold Rush, as with all the other rushes, newspapers created a picture of an easy and comfortable trip to the mines. One Whatcom publication even stated that "you could ride a bicycle to the mines." This was, of course, a fabrication and prospective miners learned the hard truth of it upon their arrival at Loop's, where all forms of wheeled traffic halted. From there the movement of supplies and people continued by horse, mule, or on human backs.

Onward to the Fields of Gold

Leaving Loop's, the trail contoured up the north side of the river, crossed Boulder Creek, then dropped down to the Nooksack. At this location, a prospector forded half of the river to the lower end of McDonald's Island, traveled up the island and then crossed to the other side of the Nooksack. Herman Steiner, who in 1893 homesteaded on the land east of McDonald's Island, operated a flat ferry from the top of the island to the mainland in flood stage. Steiner was also a prospector with claims up Wells Creek and later worked for the Lone Jack by pioneering routes to the mine over Mamie Pass and Swamp Creek.

The 1897 trail followed up the south side of the river from Steiner's, with much of the way over swampy ground and eventually reached Cornell's Ranch, the last outpost of civilization. After Cornell's ranch, but before the onset of the State Trail, the prospector had to ford Glacier Creek, which, at different times, could be fatally dangerous.

The somewhat improved State Trail went east along the south side of the river (the trail followed part of what today is the Deadhorse Road) and then crossed the North Fork just down from Thompson's Falls (later named Nooksack Falls). The mileage of the State Trail from the Glacier Creek crossing to the Thompson's Falls ford was about six miles. The trail continued east on the northern side of the river until it reached Gold Hill, a tent camp.

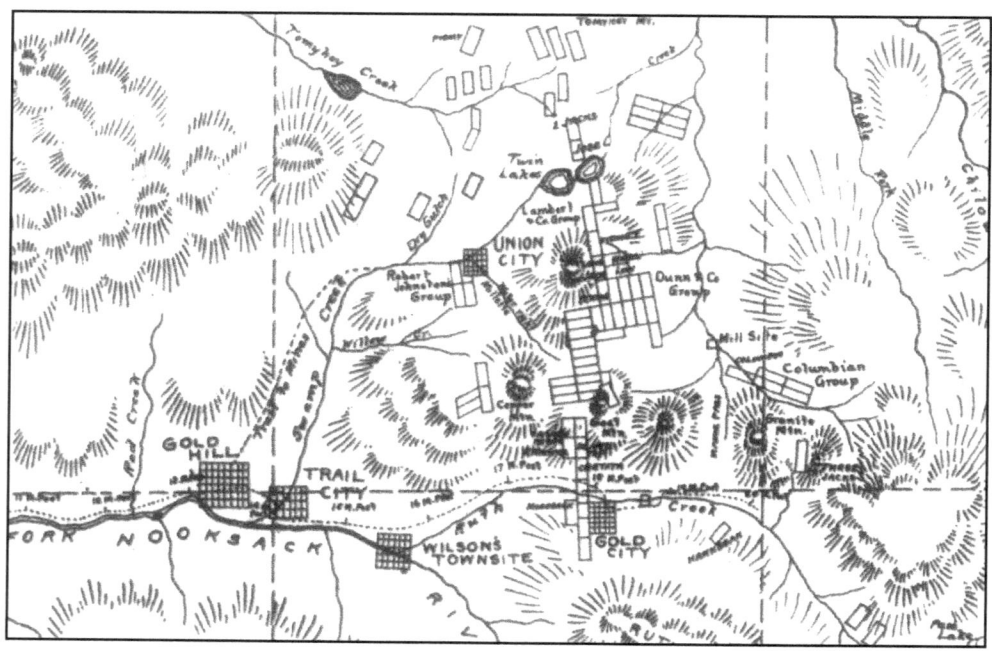

Map of claims around Twin Lakes. (J. Munroe).

A short distance beyond—at the location where Swamp Creek emptied into the North Fork, the prospector found another camp, named Trail City, and the beginning of yet another, final trail to Twin Lakes and the Lone Jack.

The State Wagon Road continued up the North Fork to the mouth of Ruth Creek and then followed Ruth Creek up to milepost 20, which was the location of Barber Camp. (Barber Camp was located in the area of the current horse camp at the end of Hannegan Pass Road and the start of the Ruth Creek Trail.) As in all developing mining districts, the area quickly became dotted with proposed town sites and tenting camps following the discovery of gold. Gold Hill was the first camp up the valley located at milepost 13.5 and became the gold rush town of Shuksan. (Gold Hill was located where the Washington State Department of Transportation Maintenance Facilities is presently located on the Mt. Baker Highway.) Trail City, a smaller camp, was located at the intersection of Swamp Creek and the North Fork while Wilson Townsite was at the intersection of Ruth Creek and the North Fork. Gold City lay up Ruth Creek directly south of Goat Mountain.

The last camp was Union City, located up Swamp Creek below the final climb to Twin Lakes. In its prime, Union City had a few cabins—the most noted being Blonden Cabin named after the discoverer of the Blonden Mine—and in this flat area today one can still locate rusted cans and glass. None of these camps, other than Shuksan, was ever developed and the town of Shuksan lasted only a few years.

Judge John Broyles

In 1894, "Judge" John Broyles and his wife arrived in Whatcom. He was defined as a judge but no one knew how he'd acquired that title. Broyles was past middle age but determined to homestead on government land in complete isolation from civilization.

After searching up the North Fork, Broyles squatted on 160 acres in the heart of the unsurveyed wilderness. Before he had time to establish or prove up on his claim as a homesteader, all of his claim and the surrounding land was withdrawn from homesteading and brought into the Government Forest Reserve. Soon the federal government tried to remove Broyles from his claim, but the old "Judge" refused to budge. Thus began the long struggle between homesteader Broyles and the U.S. Land Office, wherein the "Judge" used every power and influence, both legal and political, to defend his forest home.

Meanwhile, by 1897, right in the middle of the fight with government over his rightful property, a second conflict arose. With the rush in full tempo, prospectors were attempting to settle on his proposed land claim and went so far as to form the town of Gold Hill. With no proof of ownership, Broyles was having a difficult struggle keeping these people off what he felt was his property.

Birdwell's toll bridge at Nooksack Falls. (J. Steiner)

The township's name changed from Gold Hill to Shuksan overnight. A post office was created May 12, 1898 and lasted until Aug. 15, 1899 with John Treutle as postmaster. Permanent structures started being built in the spring of 1898. By the end of the year, Shuksan boasted of having a boarding house, a restaurant, two stores (one owned by John Treutle), and 20 cabins, all thrown together to service the rush.

"Judge" Broyles, perhaps seeing the folly in trying to keep these people off his land, decided instead to join them and cash in where he could. In 1903, he renamed the town Herman and the Herman Post Office remained opened from April 15, 1903 to Oct. 30, 1907, with Broyles as postmaster. During the rush, Broyles also constructed the Broyles Hotel at Trail City. However Trail City soon folded and the hotel was abandoned like many others during that time.

Broyles finally received outright ownership of the land in 1914, winning his case on an old statute. By then, the rush was finished and the town of Gold Hill/Shuksan/ Herman had died. Broyles died in 1918 and once again the ownership of the property was up in the air. D.C. Gates, representing the Mt. Baker Development Co. that developed the Mt. Baker Lodge, purchased the land through the estate and some trading followed that, in the end, returned "Judge" Broyles' land to the federal government.

Chaotic Beginnings and the Formation of the District

As the years went on, the roads and trails remained in terrible condition and improvements were slow to come. The area, which later became known as the Mt. Baker National Forest, was a federal no-man's land. Neither the federal government nor any other governmental body had any form of control over what went on. With this lack of control, there weren't any provisions to provide money or support for its development. A group of miners repeatedly petitioned the county to step forward and help, but these and other requests were rejected.

Gradually though, the county did improve the main road as far as the beginning of the (proposed) Cascade Wagon Road. By 1899, all major crossings of streams and rivers on the State Trail had been bridged. In May of that year, the trail was widened to a wagon road as far as the bridge below Nooksack Falls where the construction of a power plant, later named Excelsior Powerhouse, was proposed. Labor on the trail project above Nooksack Falls was being performed by claim owners who, under mining laws, could perform the required site assessment work on their claims by building or working on the trail leading to the district.

On Dec.7, 1897 Matt Birdwell petitioned the Whatcom County commissioners for the right to build a toll bridge across the North Fork directly down-stream from the Nooksack Falls for the purpose of providing a safe passage over the extremely dangerous crossing. The vote passed and the commissioners allowed toll rates of: "foot passengers, 10 cents; man and horse, 25 cents; loose or pack animals, either cattle or horses, 15 cents."

The bridge was constructed over the winter of 1897. The county commissioners supported the needed project, but they had no control over its construction because it was in a "no man's" land. The county thus provided no means of financial support.

At the time of the Mount Baker Mining District Rush, Canadian prospectors were experiencing the same level of mining intensity north

Newspaper ad. (J. Munroe)

of the border. The location of the border crossing was an item of zero importance and neither Americans nor Canadians paid any concern to it. At this time, only a few knew where it actually was.

An example would be Silesia Creek, on the American side, which drained north to the Chilliwack River in Canada, and further down to the Fraser River. Prospectors, when finding a claim near the border, were undecided whether to file with the United States or with Canada. Also because of this early development on the Canadian side, an alternate route was created to obtain access into the district. The distance was longer, but the trail eliminated the high pass at Twin Lakes.

Someone needed to create order. The Mount Baker Mining District formed in Sumas in the spring of 1898 with a membership of 55. It was originally named the Nooksack Mining District—a name that was changed following the first meeting of council. The members were miners, mine owners, and mine operators. In those days, self-government was typical of areas where intensive mining was being performed.

The newly formed district created a constitution, by-laws and standing committees for its members. The boundaries were created as follows: 1) The Mount Baker Mining District would begin at the northwest corner of the town of Sumas, and run due south to a point due west of the summit of

Mt. Baker; 2) It would extend east over the summit of Mt. Baker to the Skagit River; 3) Then follow the Skagit in a northerly direction to the Canadian Border; and 4) Finish in a line due west along the boundary line to the point of beginning.

On July 1, 1907, a revised group of 25 members reorganized the Mount Baker Mining District and filed the necessary papers in Whatcom County Courthouse. The main reason for the change was to increase the size of the district. One of the first items of business of the newly-formed council was the selection of ore from the Mt. Baker and the Slate Creek Districts to be displayed at the Lewis and Clark Fair in Portland the following summer. The ore for the fair was eventually provided by James Cady from the Slate Creek District, R.S. Lambert from the Twin Lakes/Red Mountain Regions, and F.M. Lewis from the Great Excelsior belt.

Two old prospectors, Amos Zimmer, left and Bert Lowry. (J. Steiner)

The First Winter

With the rush creating an enormous level of activity in the fall of 1897 and the following year of 1898, Whatcom County became a sea of incredible growth. Men were flooding in from all over the country to obtain a shot at this easy gold rush, publicized everywhere to be readily accessible. Little did they know of the terrain, weather, and winter in the North Cascades.

In 1897, a large number of prospectors were returning from the Klondike and it was natural for the ones with nothing to show for their effort to want to attempt one more shot at riches in the Mount Baker Mining District. Prospectors, arriving daily into Sumas on the B.B. & B.C. Railway, were soon followed by merchants, then saloon keepers, girls of the night, packers, claims and real-estate sellers, businessman seeking established claims, and last came the con-men and swindlers.

By the time the snow settled in the winter of 1897, between 800 to 1,000 prospectors were estimated to be in the district, 400 alone camped at Twin Lakes. Then, within a few short days, they were gone. A long winter with up to 25 feet of snow reclaimed the land. All was still except the sound of wind and the district was closed for another year.

Staking Claims

At the time of discovery of the Lone Jack, all prospecting in Washington State was under the direction of the Mineral Location Federal Law of 1872. All valuable mineral deposits in the lands belonging to the United States—surveyed or unsurveyed—were "public domain" and open for mining by citizens and by aliens who had declared their intent to become citizens.

Forest Reserve Land also fell into this classification. When a prospector was the first in an area approximately the size of a claim, the area became his sole right for searching under the protection of a doctrine called *Pedis Possession*. So long as he remained in possession continuously and diligently worked his area, no other prospector could enter for prospecting purposes. *Pedis Possession* protected prospectors from forcible, fraudulent, or clandestine intrusion and so, in many mining districts, the *Pedis Possession* doctrine became an item of disputes.

A documented discovery was essential to receiving a claim or a location. An official "discovery" required that minerals had been found and that "evidence is (was) of such a character that a person of ordinary prudence would be justified in the further expenditure of his labor and means, with a reasonable prospect of success, in developing a valuable mine." After a discovery, the land upon which the discovery was made was temporarily removed from the public domain and the discoverer was protected in his possession during the time allowed for the performance of location work. An approved claim, once issued, conclusively established that a claim of land was valuable for mineral purposes, and thereafter the fact of the discovery was no longer open to question.

With the Mount Baker Mining District lobbying to Whatcom County, the county agreed to appoint the Maple Falls *Leader* publisher Henry Strickfaden to act as the regional office of the county auditor for the purpose of recording mining claims in 1899. His proximity to the district provided a real assistance in the recording of claims.

Federal Law limits a lode claim to 600 feet by 1,500 feet with 1,500 feet along the vein and 300 feet either side of the vein. The measurements are to be made horizontally, without regards to the contour of the land. The proper sequence to locate a claim in Washington is 1) Make a lode discovery, 2) Post the location notice, 3) Stake corners and mark boundaries, and 4) Record location notice. The discoverer shall locate his claim by posting at the discovery at the time of discovery a notice containing the name of lode, name of the locator and the date of discovery. Included a brief description of the ground also the distance claimed on either side of the vein. The location notice should be posted at or as near as possible to the point of discovery. The notice should be mounted on a post, stump, tree, or monument of stone. The notice should be easily found, and be readable. The notice should be sealed in a jar or a sealed can. The staking of the claim, which is the marking of the surface

boundaries, is by placing substantial posts or stone bearing the name of the lode and date of location. One post or monument must appear at each corner of such claim. Such post or monument must not be less than three feet high; if posts are used they shall be not less than four inches in diameter and shall be set in the ground in a substantial manner. If a claim is located on ground that is covered wholly or in part with brush or trees, such brush shall be cut and trees be marked or blazed along the lines of such claim to indicate the location of such lines. The sidelines of the claims may be straight, segmented, or curved however the end lines must be parallel. If one or more corners of the claim are so inaccessible to an experienced climber that an attempt to reach them would endanger his life, the use of a witness stake is permissible.

The discoverer of a lode shall, within ninety days from the date of discovery, record in the office of the county auditor of the county in which such lode is found, a notice containing the name or names of the locators, the date of location, the number of feet in length, claimed on each side of the discovery, the general course of the lode, and such a description of the claim or claims located by reference to some natural object or permanent monument as will identify the claim. In order for a claim to be readily identifiable the claim name should be included. In the State of Washington the recording of a location notice is essential to a valid location.

Mill site claims can be made and have no mineral value in character. The mill site claim cannot be placed in the area of the lode or vein to give the owners added mining area. The mill site claim cannot exceed five acres in size however there is no limitation to its shape. Another type of claim is a tunnel site claim. This claim is used to provide tunnel accessibility, which is not upon the mining claim.

The annual assessment work requires one hundred dollars worth of labor performed each year from September 1 to September 1. Upon a failure to comply with these requirements the claim or mine upon which such failure occurred shall be open to relocation in the same manner. The work must be performed in good faith and must tend to develop the claims and facilitate the extraction of ore. Failure to perform assessment work may result in forfeiture of the claim. There is no forfeiture unless and until there is relocation. The building of road counts toward assessment work provided its purpose is to facilitate development of the claim and extraction of ore. Aerial tramway to haul ore is valid work. Construction or repair of mills and smelters are not classified as assessment work. Tool house and a blacksmith shop are approved however a cabin is not. The expense of keeping a watchman on the property was approved where his services were necessary to preserve building and equipment however not when the watchman was to warn off prospectors. After assessment work is completed, an affidavit must be filed 30 days after September 1, or before. This affidavit shall be made and recorded in the office of the county auditor of the county. Such affidavit shall state the exact amount and kind

Mountain Home Hotel built in Glacier in 1904. (M. Impero)

of labor including the number of feet of shaft, tunnel, or open cut made of such claim. Such affidavit shall contain the section, township, and range. During periods of national emergency, Congress has seen fit to suspend the assessment work. The duty to perform annual assessment work continues until the payment of the purchase price for patent land to the Federal Government.

The steps in a patent mining claim procedure start with a survey by a licensed Deputy United States Mineral Surveyor. The applicant must pay the surveyor's fees and charges. After the survey, an application for patent must be filed. The statutory requires development work to the amount of five hundred dollars per claim. As part of the patent application proceedings, a copy of the plat of the survey of land for which application for patent has been made must be posted conspicuously upon the claims involved and notice must be published in the county in which the lands are located. A procedure exists for anyone to contest the rights of the applicant to obtain a patent. Upon issuance of a patent, the patentee acquires full title to the land patented, including all surface rights, timber, and minerals.

Developing a Claim

Following the initial rush of prospector activity came the period of claim development. By 1902, prospecting continued to be done in the Mount Baker Mining District, but the bulk of the activity now focused on developing the claims that had been proven to have financial value.

Enough claims had been discovered that the business world of Whatcom County felt a genuine boost in its economy. Maple Falls, Kendall, and Glacier were expanding on a daily basis, reflecting the amazing growth experienced by the whole North Fork Drainage. Without the mining district and the need for heavy machinery for the Excelsior Powerhouse, the expansion of the B.B. & B.C. Railroad and its arrival in Glacier might never have happened.

After discovery of a potential claim, the discoverer had the option of developing the claim or selling the claim to investors. A standard practice of the discoverer was to high grade the ore samples and have these samples taken to an assayer of his choice, who would create an over-rated value.

Grasett & Co. one of the first banks in Whatcom to handle gold dust. (J. Munroe)

Next, if a group of developers became interested in said claim, they would direct their own mining engineer to acquire samples from the discovery and these samples went to their own chosen assayer. The mining engineer's review of the site included a thorough evaluation of mineral richness as well as the potential for milling at a proposed site. Both developers and investors used this information to make decisions concerning which claims to develop.

The accessibility to a mine for construction and operation played a major factor in determining the feasibility of a proposed operation. The Silver Tip Mine, located on a hillside above Ruth Creek along which a proposed extension of the B.B. & B.C. Railroad, lay up Ruth Creek and over Hannegan Pass—all the way to Eastern Washington. Yet with the proposed railroad built, all the freighting, construction and operation of the Silver Tip Claim would have been a great deal easier than at an isolated mine similar to the Lone Jack or an even more isolated mine such as

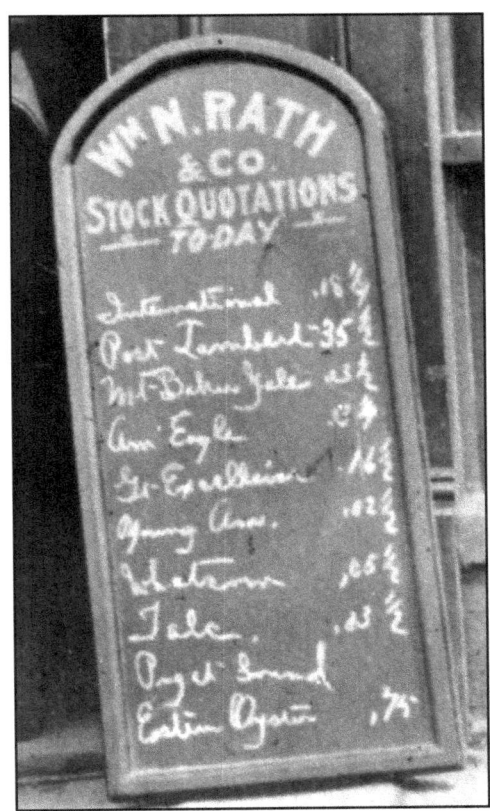

Rath & Co. stock quotations. (J. Munroe)

Rath & Co., brokers of mining claims. (J. Munroe)

the Boundary Red Mill—located on Red Mountain on a very steep hillside looking down on the Chilliwack River. Furthermore, the Silver Tip could have shipped the concentrated ore on the railroad, saving them the trouble of milling it on site. With all of these advantages, the Silver Tip Mine could have been a great success. Unfortunately for them, the B.B. & B.C. never constructed their railroad to this point.

Once a developer group had taken legal control over a claim or mine, the group formed a company. The company then sold stock to provide funding. By 1902, the Mount Baker Mining District played host to 20 or more companies actively raising money for the development and operation of mines. Development had begun on the Great Excelsior Mine, the Lone Jack, the Golden Dawn, the Copper King, the Terra Alta, the Ruth Creek Falls Mine, the Silver Tip, the American Eagle, the Lone Star, the Gold Run Mining and Milling (Gargett Brothers), and the Boundary Red Mountain Mine. In the end, only three of this list actually shipped gold or gold ore: the Lone Jack, The Great Excelsior, and the Boundary Red Mountain. Boundary Red, despite its isolation, proved to be the largest shipper.

MASS-MEETING

TO-NIGHT

Monday, Sept. 20th, 8:00 P. M.

AT THE CITY HALL

To devise means to make BELLINGHAM BAY the only base of supplies for

WHATCOM GOLD MINES

Reach the Silicia Creek Mines from Bellingham Bay only.

BUSINESS MEN UNITE!

Now is the time to strike for the trade in the dawn of the stampede.

EVERY BUSINESS MAN COME!

Whatcom Board Trade and Citizens.

Typical flier to promote the gold rush. (WWU-CPNWS)

Mine Brokers

The E.Y. Grasett & Co., Bankers, in Whatcom, Washington, was one of the first to bargain in gold dust or gold bars. Grasett & Co. published an advertisement that indicated that they were capable of assaying ore and gold dust in their office by their in-house mining engineer—a man "of many years' experience in this area." The advertisement further referred to the Mount Baker Mining District as "Whatcom County's Klondike." E.Y. Grasett & Co. along with others, attempted to catch the attention of prospectors and capitalists before they undertook the expensive and hazardous journey to the Alaskan Gold Fields.

The Wm. N. Rath & Co. also of New Whatcom, dealt in mine brokerage as well. A reader-board, captured in a 1902 photograph of the Wm. N. Rath & Co. office, lists the then-current price for local mining stocks. Amongst 10 other mines, the Lone Jack lists at 35½ cents per share and the Great Excelsior at 16$^{1}/_{5}$ cents per share. These prices reflected the stocks' worth before either mine initiated operation.

In 1903, a daily column titled "Mines & Mining in the Northwest" appeared in one of Bellingham's newspapers, *The Daily Reveille*. On every third day, the column specifically covers the mines of the Mount Baker Mining District. Commonplace mining news appeared in this column while major news—things like big start-ups or sales—surfaced as front-page stories. At this time, almost all of the citizens of Whatcom County wanted to see development in the area, and eagerly awaited news of it in the papers.

The Great Nooksack Mining Co. Scam

Like all mining districts, the Mount Baker Mining District had its fair share of swindlers. Honest citizens ran a few of them off at night, like a man named St. John who jumped claims in the Twin Lakes area. The biggest and most successful scam belonged to the Nooksack Mining Co., which created a bogus operation at the Nooksack Mine—a fiasco that went down in history as one of the most elaborate shams at the turn of the century in Washington or Alaska.

In 1900, a small group of men quietly staked a group of claims on the west side of Sumas Mountain east of the town of Nooksack. C.F. Bernard and J. Swinehart recorded the seven claims that made up the Nooksack Mining Co. as the Mystic, Old Tom, the Bellboy, the Shoo Fly, the Yum Yum, the Last Chance, and the Lucky Boy.

Strangely, the men in charge constructed a stamp mill and a complex of buildings almost before even they sank the mineshafts. By the time three shafts operated—including ore carts and a rail system—they had also constructed a hotel, a dance hall, several bunkhouses and a large framed office building. The old sourdoughs questioned the activities at the new mine, but few people were welcome to the site while the operation progressed, and most of the information came as rumor.

The Nooksack Mining Co. further gathered the old sourdoughs' interest when a regular stage route opened between the Nooksack Mine, Bellingham Bay and Sumas. The stagecoaches began transporting full loads of visitors to the Nooksack Mine, luggage and all. Most of the visitors were strangers to the area and later learned to be representatives of future investors in the Nooksack Mine from Seattle, San Francisco, New York, Ohio, Florida, and a multitude of other places. They came on behalf of their investors to investigate the mine, its operation, and to see its gold firsthand.

While the representatives were at the site, they enjoyed hospitality that included a hotel room, an elegant menu, a well-stocked bar, a dance hall with a round imported oak floor and female companionship, all on the tab of the Nooksack Mining Co. During their visit, the representatives toured the carriage house and the office building, and saw the bags of gold packed in the vault.

As the clincher, they then descended into the mine itself. Here, guides held lanterns to the cavern walls, displaying the rich glow of gold embedded therein. Surely this was the most elaborate gold mine in the west, the guests must have thought, and very few left without wanting to own a part of it.

Mining prospect at east Twin Lake. (J. Christenson)

The Nooksack Mining Co. managed to run a combination gold mine and resort for more than two years before attracting some serious local attention. Curiosity about the operation got the best of a well-known miner from Sumas, who one night slipped into one of the shafts and removed a sample of ore. The results of an assay performed the next day revealed that the ore was practically worthless.

The investigator, smelling a rat, took his information directly to the courthouse. As soon as the scandal emerged, an unusual thing happened. The men in charge of the Nooksack Mine granted their employees some time off, shut the mill down, and locked the buildings. Then they flew by night.

The operation never ran again and the years that followed saw many lawsuits filed. The company went into receivership and mint records showed that no gold ever came out of the mine. In fact, geological reports on the Nooksack mine site showed it to be barren of any gold at all. To create their illusion, the mine walls had been salted. Somebody had taken a shotgun shell and replaced the shot with gold flecks, and then fired it into the walls of the mine. The only consolation for the hundreds of investors was that they hadn't been taken by some two-bit crook or ordinary swindler.

On Feb. 17, 1906, the Whatcom County Courthouse in Bellingham held a sale of all assets of the Nooksack Mine and brought in a total amount of $395, then divided this amount among 33 listed creditors. Of the 370 stockholders, not a one received a dime for their investment.

Chapter 4

Early Development

The Word Gets Out

Post, Van Valkenburg, and Lambert all sat down at Lambert's Sumas law office following the return of Post and Van Valkenburg from the newly discovered claim. The first item of business was to form a three-member partnership wherein each partner received an equal share. The claims had been filed separately to each of the three. However, by combining their claims in a partnership, the overall value could be increased numerous times over.

Based on his many years of experience, Post reasoned that potential buyers would be soon arriving from all parts of the country for an opportunity to buy out their valued claims. Post reasoned further that, due to the isolation of the area, the development of the Lone Jack would be extremely expensive and time consuming. Lambert and Van Valkenburg also knew that Post's interest level in the project would be quickly lost as he had similarly lost interest in many of his previous projects.

As if to prove their suspicions, Post was already talking of returning into the mountains, where he felt certain that a larger and richer discovery awaited him. Because the ore samples they'd hand-picked had been assayed at $3,750 per ton, the partnership

could hang back and prepare to review and select the best proposal. With all their documents in place, Lambert and Van Valkenburg returned to life in Sumas, while Post quickly returned to the mountains.

For Lambert and Van Valkenburg, life continued far from normal, as the talk about town, county, and the state was that of their discovery. People flooded into Lambert's office, not for legal advice but to discuss the Lone Jack. The *Blade* and *Reveille,* the newspapers in Whatcom, dispatched reporters to interview the two. The editor of the Sumas News came calling daily to get the latest information, assuming somehow that there was more to give.

As foreseen by the partnership, the news of their find had spread quickly. With the coming of winter, a variety of investors and developers had arrived at the newly formed Mount Baker Mining District. The strike was quickly predicted by national newspapers to be larger than the Klondike Discovery of one year earlier, and further favored for being closer to civilization than Dawson City.

On Oct. 2, 1897, Post led a group headed up by Mr. Davis of San Francisco into the site. Mr. Davis represented the B.B.I. and the B.B. &

B.C. Railroad. The first of winter snow had blanketed Bear Mountain, and the site would soon be covered with up to 20 feet of snow.

Henry Stanislawsky, of a Portland, Ore. firm, left a meeting with Henry Hahn and Leo Friede after discussing their interests in the Lone Jack claims. His plan called for travel to Sumas by train and then to join with Post for a guided journey to the mine by pack train and on foot. Little did he realize that the proposed pack train would only take him the first half of the trip, and that he would travel the rest on foot.

Post, Stanislawsky, a Colorado gold-miner named Harry Trimble, and Van Valkenburg headed out for the trip to the Lone Jack. Upon their return, the group appeared exhausted and tattered out. When newspaper reporters questioned Stanislawsky concerning the claims, he stated, "These claims are in the most isolated area I have ever seen. The area is extremely steep and with glaciers of ice above it. The trail going to the location is at this time totally obliterated and in some locations one is not able to locate it at all." He additionally stated that he felt that the claims were intensely rich.

On Nov. 25, 1897, Stanislawsky and Trimble returned to Portland with the news of their survey and examination of the Lone Jack claims.

The First Proposals

In two short days that followed, Sumas received word by telegram that Hahn of Portland, Ore. chose to purchase all the claims of the Lone Jack. On Nov. 29, 1897, Lambert forwarded to Hahn in Portland a proposal letter with two options to purchase.

In the first proposal, Lambert offered a total price of $50,000 with $2,000 upon signing, $3,000 on July 1, 1898, $10,000 on Jan. 1, 1899, $10,000 on July 1, 1899, and $10,000 on Jan. 1, 1900. The balance or last payment was to be paid after Jan. 1, 1900 by depositing 25 percent of the net earnings or cleanup from the mill. This would be paid after all other monthly expenses had been paid.

In the second option, again the total price would be $50,000 but this time the payments were to come from 10 percent of the monthly cleanups with the final payment to be received on Jan. 1, 1902.

All three partners, along with their wives, signed this option letter. No record shows for sure which option was picked. However, indications are that option No. 1 was used. The number of offers the three received was unknown but the partners apparently had a preset amount and received this or more from Hahn.

On March 10, 1898, Hahn, president of the Portland Chamber of Commerce, incorporated under the laws of the State of Oregon the Mt. Baker Mining Co. with Friede and Stanislawsky. Hahn was elected president with Friede elected vice president.

On Sept. 2 of the same year, Hahn entered into a contract with the Mt. Baker Mining Co. and assigned to the new company an optional contract to purchase the Post, Lambert, and Van Valkenburg claims. In this assignment, Mt. Baker Mining Co. agreed to discharge all present and future liabilities imposed upon Hahn. The price paid by Mt. Baker Mining Co. to Hahn totaled $90,000. With this single legal action Hahn profited approximately $40,000 and the Mt. Baker Mining Co. prepared marketing shares to all potential shareholders.

On Dec. 5, 1899, the Mt. Baker Mining and Milling Co. was incorporated in the State of Washington by F.M. Irons, Martin Pfluke, and Ernest Irons. This Washington State corporation had no relationship or connection with the Mt. Baker Mining Co. of Portland, Ore.

In a mining deed dated March 23, 1901, title transferred from Post, Lambert, and Van Valkenburg to the Mt. Baker Mining Co. The total ownership of the Lone Jack from the three partners transferred after receiving a total of $40,000. Why the $50,000 as stated in the sale agreement was not received will be lost to history, though the possibility remains that a part of the $50,000 was taken as shares of stock by one or more of the sellers. Post, after the final payment, commenced to build a new residence in Sumas. At a later date, Lambert wound up being one of the largest shareholders in the Mt. Baker Mining Co.

Legal Disputes Arise

Legal problems plagued the Lone Jack Mine from the beginning. Being first in a newly created gold rush area, one would have thought that they would have been free of problems for a period of time. But they were not so lucky. Using hindsight, it is not hard to tell that many of the early problems could have been avoided.

After the signing of the initial agreement between the claimholders and Hahn, John McClellan made suit that he had been wrongly dismissed as a middleman in the deal between the parties. His complaint stated that he was directed to Sumas to investigate, at the request of Hahn, if the Lone Jack discovery was for sale. McClellan had then reported back that it was, and in turn received $40 from Hahn for his service.

Following that act, he then alleged to have been retained by Post and Lambert to act as the middleman in the negotiations between the two parties. No claim was filed against Hahn, the Mt. Baker Mining Co. or against Van Valkenburg because he was said not to be present and no part of the deal. The Superior Court of Whatcom County ruled a judgment on Jan. 27, 1903, in favor of the plaintiff John McClellan for $4,000 to be paid by Post and Lambert. The Court ruled that McClellan is entitled to 10 percent of the total reduced sale, a settlement that ended up being $40,000.

Early Plans for a Stamp Mill

Henry Stanislawsky, specified then as manager of the Mt. Baker Mining Co. operation, stated the company planned to be installing a 10-stamp ore crushing and recovery mill next year, as soon as 1898. Post, upon returning from the Hahn & Co. office in Portland, gave word that he'd been directed as superintendent in the fully crewed construction of a road up Swamp Creek to provide access to the mine, with work soon to commence. Also, Lambert stated, "The company soon will make extensive improvements in the way of road building from the 18-mile post to the head of Swamp Creek."

In March 1898, Stanislawsky returned to Sumas with two mining experts and horse packers who were preparing to transport five tons of provisions to the mine site. Stanislawsky, a mining expert, had years of experience in different mining districts throughout the West; however, the Lone Jack was his first in the North Cascades. The winters in this area lasted an extremely long time and the 6,000-foot level, where the Lone Jack was located, could accumulate snow any month of the year. In most cases the snow lasted at the mine site until July and in some cases all year long. Stanislawsky appears to have arrived approximately four months too early.

Stanislawsky Cabin, first structure built in the area of The Lone Jack. (J. Munroe)

On June 4, 1898, Stanislawsky, representing the Mt. Baker Mining Co. was camped at Silesia Creek, which is in the drainage system directly below the mine site. The mine site was located approximately three-quarters of a mile away and 4,000 feet higher. Of the five tons of supplies he'd started out with in March, only 1,500 pounds remained.

The group constructed a cabin that would later be known as "Stanislawsky Cabin" and which served as a base for operations in 1898. This cabin was located on a small ridge above Silesia Creek in the only location they could find that was not directly in an avalanche chute while also high enough to be above the flood-plain of Silesia Creek.

Unfortunately for them, the location of the cabin and the mine were a long distance apart.

After being joined at the cabin site by Trimble and Friede, the other two owners of the operation, the three returned to Whatcom on July 30. They announced their current plan to scout out a new proposed route in from Canada—a trail leading up the Chilliwack River to reach Silesia Creek and the mine, hoping to eliminate the high pass area of Twin Lakes.

The owners felt using the Canadian route in lieu of the North Fork of the Nooksack River route created a more moderate route. With the cooperation of the Canadian government, it would

Lone Jack Trail, location of where the Silesia Trail intersects. (J. Munroe).

Lone Jack Trail at the upper Twin Lake. (J. Munroe)

accelerate the construction of the mill and all other facilities as needed. The owners were hopeful that the proposed mill installation could still be completed that year. What these owners did not realize or elected to ignore were the restrictions placed on all materials and men crossing the border back into the United States, not to mention the duty laid on the gold ore as it was moved.

The summer of 1898 found the mountains alive with prospectors from all over the United States. The sound of dynamite blasting remained constant, as did the flow of people coming and going. A small town with tents and other temporary structures was thrown up on the flat land surrounding the Twin Lakes

Basin. At one point, this tent city became the largest voting contingency, named Hannegan precinct, in eastern Whatcom County with a population of about 200 to 300 miners. By Russ Lambert's estimation, there were 600 men in the Mining District, all of whom would be gone with the arrival of winter.

By late August, the company had initiated work on tunnels or adits into the Lone Jack. One had reached 75 feet, the other about 100 feet, and a third adit had been started at the Lulu Site. A trail from the Stanislawsky Cabin to the mine had also been completed.

At the mine adit portal, a building serving as a cookhouse, bunkhouse,

First Lone Jack digging. (WWU-CPNWS)

Early mining engineer inside Lone Jack. (J. Munroe)

41

storehouse, and blacksmith shop had been constructed in such a position that avalanches of any type would miss it. With a crew of 15 men working, about six would enter and work in the mine and the remaining crew would stay on the outside attending to other improvement needs. All packing and foot traffic, at that time, came and went on the somewhat completed trail from the Canadian side.

By the first of November of that year, the exterior labor force had ceased working as planned and had left the men inside the mine to continue working all winter long. One day in December, the crew returned out of the adit at the close of the workday to discover that the whole complex of the building had been swept away by avalanches except the far end, which served as the cookhouse. The men became gravely concerned for the fate of the cook. In digging through the debris, they located the poor man hiding in a corner, scared for his life that another slide would come crashing down.

The group spent a cold and miserable night huddled together for warmth and at daylight left as quickly as possible. It was a long day's journey to reach Shuksan, where only a couple of winter watchmen remained and were able to take them in.

The spring of 1899 became a period of reorganization for the owners of the Lone Jack and manager Henry Stanislawsky. The enormous task of developing the Lone Jack in its desolate location had become a major item of discussion in the office of Mt. Baker Mining Co. The planned project of installing a stamp mill appeared to be off by years. With the setback the destroyed building caused in December, the severity and the length of the winter had become a greater concern. Mt. Baker Mining Co. owners must have reluctantly started asking themselves if they had made a sound decision in buying the mine.

First bunk/cook house with blacksmith shop at Lone Jack. (Bellingham Herald)

Bunk/cook house with blacksmith shop after being hit with a snow avalanche. (Bellingham Herald)

In early 1899, the Canadian government initiated work in building a road east from Chilliwack City to the national boundary, a distance of 22 to 25 miles. In April, Stanislawsky's crew worked clearing the company trail from the border to the mine. The completion of the county road from Loop's Ranch above Maple Falls to Glacier was finally concluded as well.

Patented Claims

The Lone Jack, Lulu, Whist, Jennie, and Sidney mines were surveyed under Mineral Survey No. 534, patent No. 37,604 dated January 4, 1900. The Jennie Claim measured 600 feet by 1,500 feet and was rectangular in size while the others were all odd sizes and shapes. The plat showed all improvements such as adits (tunnels), trails, and cabins. All the completed improvements were listed as:

General Improvement #1
   30 miles of pack trail costing $2,000

Lulu Improvement #1
   tunnel 5'x6'x116' costing $1,856

Lone Jack
   Improvement #1
   tunnel 5'x6'x30' costing $480
   Improvement #2
   tunnel 5'x6'x20' costing $320
   Improvement #3
   excavation 20'x70' costing $500
   Improvement #4
   cabin 16'x45' costing $500
   Improvement #5
   blacksmith shop $50

The improvements totaled $5,706

The trail construction shown on the plat dropped down to Silesia Creek and onward to Canada. The survey, and all future surveys, were made using United States Land Monument No. 1 as the reference point.

The Mt. Baker Mining Co. applied to the federal government in Washington, D.C. for patent rights on the five mining claims that made up the Lone Jack or Post-Lambert. Their approval, which was held up in the beginning, was granted from the federal office on Dec. 31, 1903, and the letter was signed by President T. Roosevelt, and F.M. McKean, Secretary. The document contained a full legal description of each of the claims, and was numbered General Land Office No. 37,602.

These 88 patented acres were and remain privately owned, requiring taxes be paid comparable to any other privately owned land in the county. Being within national forest lands, these patented claims were similar to others in the state. The Mt. Vernon and the Jumbo located south of the Lone Jack, are two claims which were patented on Sept. 10, 1903 and were both owned by H.B. Cupples.

English and Son, New Owner

In the *Blade,* one of the daily newspapers of Whatcom, a Sept. 12, 1899 headline read: *"The Lone Jack (Post-Lambert) Gold Mine in the Mt. Baker Mining District was sold today to English and Son of Baker City, Oregon for $150,000."* The story went on: *"Fifteen men will work the mine all winter, new owners mean*

43

business. They will dig ore from the Post-Lambert all winter, getting ready for the stamp mill, cabins built in the side of the cliff, ten stamp mills will be erected next summer which will be located on the flat about a mile below the lead (adit), a tramway will be used for getting the ore down to the mill." Also stated in a later issue: *"The new owners now have 25 men working and are paying $3.00 per day per man, which includes board, or $5.00 for man and team of horses with board for both. They will work five shifts during the winter and will employ 200 men in the spring. Merchandise can come from the Chilliwack Side or the U.S. Side. It is stated that a horse can pack in 150 to 200 lbs. on the U.S. Side trail."*

This sale was similar to the previous sale in that it was a bonded sale — part cash and part shares. Being shareholders, Lambert and Van Valkenburg were pleased with this transaction for they knew that English and Son would provide the funding and expertise to complete the operation. This event meant nothing to Post, who had not retained any shares in the mine.

In October 1899, there was a major need for improvement of the trail system. Suppliers needed the ability to reach the mine and mill sites. Outfits moved equipment from the Canadian side, the majority of which was directed to the Lone Jack. To speed matters, English and Son brought in their own freight company. At the same time construction began on a

trail from the Stanislawsky Cabin to the Lone Jack Tunnel which contained 10 switchbacks and was meant to enable horses to transport supplies to the mine.

The crew also constructed two cabins on the Lone Jack Lead at an altitude of 5,000 feet. They were safely sheltered under a cliff from future snow slides. The crew working in the adit reported high-grade seams, four to six feet wide, reaching approximately 250 feet down. They planned to work all winter. A very lonely and isolated location it must have been. The men worked with the knowledge that the nearest medical treatment was a fair distance away and that snow conditions could block them in for days or weeks at a time.

By the spring of 1900, the problem of transportation continued to plague the Lone Jack. Although the preferred route to the Lone Jack was from the Canadian side, the North Fork Route up the Nooksack River was routine for all of the other remaining operations in the district.

W.H. Norton, a miner representing all the members of Mount Baker Mining District, had been appointed to lobby the Whatcom County government for support in receiving funding for the trail construction. One of the problems at the time was that the existing trail and the road from Glacier to Shuksan was located in the Washington Forest Reserve — a no-man's land without a governing agent. Norton pointed out to the county officials that if they don't do something, Whatcom County could risk losing all the trade and revenue of the Mining District to the Canadian side.

Around March 20, Jack Post found himself in the town of Shuksan organizing the layout and construction of a trail from Shuksan to the Lone Jack. The population of the town had started to regroup with the coming of spring and the needed labor force arrived daily. The chief requirement for the new trail was that it be wide enough for a narrow gauge wagon or sled. It was known beforehand the area that would require the largest amount of energy and labor was between Swamp Creek and Twin Lakes. This trail section would have to be constructed with the use of numerous switchbacks cut in solid rock.

In a newspaper article dated April 17, 1900, Connors, the manager, stated that 12 men were toiling in the main adit, which was 300 feet in length, and also added that work was being done on the Lulu tunnel as far as 110 feet. Already, 150 tons of concentrated ore were stored at the site and ready to be shipped to the mill upon the completion of its construction. English and Son were expecting to spend $75,000 on machinery. Their plans included a ten stamp mill, and a 4,000 foot-long tramway capable of moving 40 tons per day. A sawmill with a capacity of 10,000 board feet per day would also be built down in a timber area near the ore mill site. About 75 men planned to be employed that summer at a wage of $2.50 per day.

By mid-June, Whatcom County announced that the county road was completed from Birdwell's bridge to the town of Shuksan, a distance of 8.5 miles. The unsurfaced roadbed was seven to eight feet in width and skirted around large trees throughout its distance. Travel could be comfortable during dry weather, though the road became impassable during periods of heavy rain. Lambert, the appointed supervisor of the Washington Forest Reserve, constantly requested improvements to the road but his pleas fell on deaf ears.

The bulk of English and Son's labor force spent their time working on the trail systems and constructing support structures. The mine couldn't be developed without reasonable roads and trails to give access for the needed equipment for the ore mill and the sawmill.

On August 28, an 18-horse pack train arrived at the mine with equipment and supplies. One item in the shipment was a number of fans driven with gas engines. After dynamite blasting within the unventilated adits going back beyond 300 feet, the smoke, dust, and bad air wouldn't clear out. Miners had been threatening to quit over this serious problem, and now, with the fans in place, the problem would be lessened.

English and Son Walks Away From Lone Jack

But then, just when things began to look better for the mine, the following article appeared in the

Watch Blade newspaper dated Sept. 20, 1900: *"English & Son of Baker City, Oregon, have released all their interest in the Lone-Jack Gold Mine in the Mount Baker Mining District, their bond option price of $350,000 being allowed to go by default. They have spent $15,000 on the property, but have taken out two and a half tons of high-grade ore, which is estimated by J.C. Treutle to contain $50,000 worth of gold. The property reverts back to Hahn & Friede of Portland, who are busy sending in supplies and making arrangements to carry on the work at the mine with renewed vigor. Prior to this announcement Connors was said to be in Portland closing the sale with Hahn & Friede but in fact he was there finding out the news that English and Son were about to default on the sale. Now Hahn & Friede regained the ownership of the mine and not with enough gain in capital to finish the development or to get it to a level for another sale."*

U.S. Border Agent's Seizure

Another fresh problem arose when a pack train was seized by border agents in October 1900, as reported by the Whatcom Reville newspaper on Oct. 2 and 5, 1900. *"A whole pack train, consisting of five horses and packs, and two half-breed drivers, was seized by the United States Customs Officers at the Post-Lambert (Lone Jack) Mine in the Mount Baker area, Friday. The two packers are charged with smuggling supplies into the United States from British Columbia.*

"This seizure is the outcome of a long series of violations of United States customs laws in the Mount Baker district. Supplies have been purchased freely on the British Columbia side and packed into the district over the Chilliwack trail. A short time ago, the customs authorities decided to put a stop to their violations of the law, and Col. Albert White, government customs inspector, took three deputies to the Post-Lambert mine a few days ago. The group waited for the arrival of the pack train at the camp, which was known to be bringing supplies, purchased in Victoria, to the miners camp at this ledge. The plan was to also arrest Henry Stanislawsky, superintendent of the mine, but, as it happened, he did not come into the district with the pack train, having remained at Chilliwack, B.C.

"The pack train arrived on Friday from Chilliwack and Col. White completed the seizure and arrest. The whole party returned to Sumas via the Swamp Creek and North Fork All-American Trail arriving in the town yesterday. One of the officers of the party states that the American trail to be in good condition and no trouble experienced in getting the animals over it. Therefore, the trail question furnished no excuse for the smuggling of supplies into the Mt. Baker District.

"The supplies and horses seized will probably be confiscated by the government and the half-breed packers who are from Chilliwack, if convicted, will be fined or imprisoned." And furthermore,

"Mr. Carlisle and W.J. Connors arrived in the city Sunday to secure the release of the two half-breed packers who were arrested with the train and Mr. Stanislawsky arrived yesterday.

"Mr. Stanislawsky expressed practically the same views to the Reveille yesterday. He characterizes the seizure as outrage on the half-breeds who were acting in ignorance of the law, and also on Hahn & Co. owners of the mine, who are responsible parties and amply able to pay the duty on their supplies if the government were to show them a plan by which it can be done. The seizure is deplorable for the reason that it has the effect of shutting down the work in the district for the winter. Mr. Stanislawsky pointed out these facts to show that there was no criminal intent in taking these supplies in from the Canadian side."

(Henry Stanislawski) "The reason for purchasing them there was due to the lack of pack train facilities on this side of the line. The Swamp Creek trail has been made passable only within the past month, and there has been no time in which to prepare for packing in from this side. Again, a snowstorm will make the Swamp Creek trail impassable and the season is now so late as to make packing over the trail extremely risky. Not only is this true, but the Chilliwack trail may be blocked by snow on almost any day now. There was not a day to be wasted but now the camp cannot be improved and made safe, and there is no way to take in supplies.

"If we purchase our supplies on this side and take them through, the Canadian officers very kindly admit them without payment of duty, but we must hire a pack train at Chilliwack. These horses can carry our goods safely to the line, but once across the border the horses are liable to seizure with all they carry by the U.S. Officers. We cannot station a pack train on this side of the line and transfer, as there is no feed for the horses. If the officers had taken an invoice of our goods at the mine and let them stay, we would have willingly paid the duty but it is an outrage to suddenly jump onto innocent packers hired by men who had no intention of evading the law and after such packing had been going on for months without hindrance or warning even.

"After this season, we hoped to take everything in by way of Swamp Creek. Next year the B.B. & B.C. Railroad extension will be in operation and we will buy all our supplies in Washington and ship by rail to Boulder Creek, by wagon to Shuksan and by pack horses up Swamp Creek to the mines before the trail is blocked by snow."

Border Disputes

The International Boundary between United States and Canada, first surveyed in 1865, was easily located from the Pacific to the foothills. But where the boundary started up and over the Cascade Mountains there was great difficulty, and disputes over the border began only a short while after the original survey.

The Boundary Red Mine, located within two years of the discovery of the Lone Jack, sat high up on the north side of Red Mountain looking directly down into Canada. In 1900, the actual location of the border was elusive but it was known to run somewhat parallel to the Chilliwack River. The discoverers of the Boundary Red Mine filed their claims in Whatcom (later Bellingham). However, they found opposition from a group of Canadian prospectors who felt that the property lay on the Canadian side and were preparing to file the claim in their own country. Adding complication, the route up and over the Swamp Creek trail was impractical for accessing the Boundary Red.

With the Boundary Red in question, talk arose as to whether the Lone Jack was in the United States or Canada. After so much development, it must have seemed impossible that the Lone Jack could have been in Canada. However, the line running up and through the mountains could be misleading. After all that the owners of the Jack had gone through, this issue must have concerned them greatly.

Following is an article from the *Whatcom Reveille* dated Oct. 19, 1900, *"Canadian surveyors accomplish nothing-the disputed mining strip is in the same status as months ago. Surveyors could not find monuments. Miners will ask United States Government's aid. The Canadian surveyors at work on the Mount Baker District quit work on Oct. 9, having failed to locate the boundary line where it effects the disputed strip of mining territory. Judge Elmon Scott received this information yesterday, by letter from Homer G. Anderson, who is now at Red Mountain. Judge Scott considers the information authentic although it contradicts the report sent out by Mr. Saviers and published in the Seattle Times and later in the Reveille. It seems the Canadian surveyors did not take astronomical observations but with the Canadian field notes of the original boundary commission as a guide, attempted to find three stone monuments described in these notes. The effort was a complete failure although the surveyor worked a week over the time allotted to him. It is now believed the monuments have disintegrated under the action of the weather in the thirty-five years since they were placed there.*

"Judge Scott says an effort will now be made to get the United States Government to take up the matter and try to locate the boundary. It should not be a very great task to locate the 49th parallel, which is firmly established by treaty as the boundary line. He would like to see the line located by a joint commission or surveying party sent out by the two governments. The matter is now in exactly the same status as it was in the early summer. The Canadian surveyors accomplished nothing whatsoever and the miners in the disputed strip have no certainty as to which country their claims are in."

At some point the matter of the location of the border was settled.

Grub Stake Suit

The Weekly Reveille, New Whatcom, Washington, reported the following on Nov. 16, 1900 *"The papers are prepared and are ready for filing in the Whatcom County Clerk's office in one of the most important mining suits ever brought in the state. John C. Treutle is the plaintiff and Hahn & Co. of Portland, the mine owners and Jack Post, R.S. Lambert and L.G. Van Valkenburg of Sumas the locators, are named as defendants. Mr. Treutle claims a one-half interest in the Lone Jack claim and one-sixth interest in the Whist, Lulu, Sidney, and Jennie located in the Mt. Baker District and commonly known as the Post-Lambert mine. The last option on these claims, which was not taken up by the holders because of this threatened suit, was for $350,000, given to English & Son of Baker City, Oregon, by the Mt. Baker Mining Co. As the Lone Jack is considered the most valuable of the five claims, the suit will probably involve over $100,000. Mr. Treutle has already made a formal demand upon all the defendants named in the papers for his alleged interest therein and it is understood they will contest the claim. The papers will be filed the first of next week if not today.*

"Mr. Treutle bases his claim for a half interest in these mines on the grounds that at the time they were located, Jack Post, the locator of the Lone Jack was using a grubstake furnished by Treutle. And that the others who assisted in locating the other four claims were also sharing in the grubstake. In July 1897, according to Mr. Treutle's story, he and William Bell, an B.B. & B.C. Railroad express agent now running between Sumas and Seattle, were prospecting in the Mt. Baker District. Bell became tired of the trip and proposed to sell his share of the supplies they had with them to Mr. Treutle. The latter consented and paid Mr. Bell for half of the stuff but later Jack Post, who with Lambert and Van Valkenburg was also prospecting in the district, offered to take Treutle's grubstake and give him half of what he discovered. An oral agreement to that effect was made between Post and Treutle and the former took the grubstake and was using it when the now famous mines were discovered. The Lone Jack was located in Post's name and he also had a third interest in the other mines. Mr. Treutle says he is also prepared to prove the fact since their discovery of the claims. Post offered to pay him for the grubstake, but he refused to accept anything other than half interest in what Post had discovered. At the time of the negotiations in Sumas between Post, Lambert, and Van Valkenburg and Henry Stanislawsky representing Henry Hahn, Stanslawsky heard of the grubstake issue and located Treutle to disscuss it. Treutle stated to Henry "He had no interest in said claims, and that Hahn should go ahead and purchase the said claims, that he wished to see the county open up, and that he was not going to file any protest and that he had no interest what so ever in said claims.

"It is also stated on good authority that a damage suit for a large amount will be brought against Mt. Baker

Mining Co. by English & Son. It will be remembered that Henry Hahn purchased the claims from Post, Lambert, Van Valkenburg and in the fall of 1899 gave English & Son an option for the purchase of the same at $350,000. English & Son then spent a large sum in developing the property, not being aware during any of the time that Mr. Treutle had an unsettled claim against the mines. This they learned shortly before the expiration of the option and refused to conclude the sale unless Treutle's claim was settled. They offered to pay down one-half in cash and the balance of the purchase price in a bank note to be drawn by Hahn & Co. when the Treutle claim had been settled, but Hahn & Co. refused to agree to this proposition and the deal fell through. It is understood that English & Son's claim for damages will be for the amount spent in developing the mine while held under their option.

"Following months of discussions and debates, an agreement of all claimed owners of the Lone Jack Mine as reported in the Blade on March 23, 1901, "A deal was consummated Thursday which will have a strong influence on the mining industry in Whatcom County. J.G. and J.C. English, W.J. Connors and Hahn & Co. of Portland, Oregon purchased all rights and title in the Post-Lambert mine in the Mount Baker Country.

"This valuable property has been allowed to remain undeveloped because a clear title has never been had before. Thursday all parties claiming an interest in the mine came

together and we are informed all differences have been settled with the result that the above gentlemen will push development work as rapidly as possible and a large force of men will be placed at work as soon as the weather will permit. A stamp mill will be placed on the ground in the spring. The capitalization of the company has been raised from $100,000 to $1,000,000. The shares of the company we understand will be placed on the market for a few friends for 50 cents a share. Mr. Connors is now in Chilliwack, B.C., looking after the company's interests, but it was impossible to learn whether he would be the manager of the company or not. Those who attended the meeting, which was held here Thursday, were W.J. Connors, R.S. Lambert, Jack Post, L.G. Van Valkenburg and O.P. Brown, representing J.C. Treutle."

Under the settlement, the English interest, together with the Portland interest, all agreed to a stock settlement adjustment and some of those locally interested will still be stockholders in the corporation. The settlement also carries an adjustment of the Treutle mining suit, which has been pending in the Superior Court of Whatcom County for some time. The stock of the corporation has been increased to a capitalization of $1,000,000 fully paid up.

The Superior Court of the State of Washington for Whatcom County, a few days after the above settlement, made a judgment in favor of the defendants and awarded to the plaintiff John Treutle no title to any of the property. A question history asks is why all of the owners reached agreement with Treutle, issued him stock or money and in a few days the court awarded him nothing? Could there have been a set-up on this suit with Treutle and his friend Jack Post working together?

Overlapping Claims

Yet another legal problem dated Feb. 17, 1902 was the complaint of L.N. St. Marie vs. Mt. Baker Mining Co. A dispute had risen over the matter of overlapping claim lines between the Jennie Claim of the Mt. Baker Mining Co. and the Appleton Claim, owned by St. Marie. This suit surfaced about the time that the Mt. Baker Mining Co. was proceeding with the application for their patent of the Lone Jack. By law, if any legal matter lay open on a patent land application, the application is tabled until the matter reaches settlement.

The plaintiff requested a total expense of $175 plus his right to the land. The Mt. Baker Mining Co. requested of the court the right to provide a bond so that the request to the federal government for the patent land could continue. There was no further record of any court action to this matter.

Bald Eagle Versus Lulu

On Sept. 24, 1897, a prospector named Frank Myers located and staked a mining claim in the Mount Baker Mining District, which he named Bald Eagle. The claim shared a boundary with the Lulu Claim, which was one of the claims owned by the Mt. Baker Mining Co. The Bald Eagle claim was a standard size claim being 600 x 1500 feet. Frank Myers, after registering his claim, sold three-quarters of the Bald Eagle to L.A. Garrison and F.S. Garrison while retaining one-quarter for himself.

When the Mt. Baker Mining Co. posted its application for patent on their claims in the Deming Prospector on Nov. 15, 1901, the owners of the Bald Eagle in reading the description of the Lulu Claim determined that a portion of said claim carried upon their claim. They determined that an area 500 x 300 feet crossed the line into the Bald Eagle Claim. Garrison Bros. and Myers filed a legal action in the Superior Court of Whatcom County and this action again halted the application of the Mt. Baker Mining Co. for their patent rights to the land.

The complaint stated that the deputy United States mineral surveyor, in surveying the five claims on the Lone Jack—a requirement of the patent land precedence—had used a corner post or monument that was placed by the original prospector approximately 50 feet out of line, thus causing a major error in the survey. The complaint stated that the defendant, the Mt. Baker Mining Co., "Willfully, maliciously, wrongfully, fraudulently, and unlawfully took up said corner post from its said position, placed and implanted it in another different and false position."

The U.S. mineral surveyor ordered a second survey of the area, However, "A heavy, unexpected and premature fall of snow, a fall of six feet in depth, made it wholly impractical to make the survey this year." Left unsettled, the matter halted any further approval of the patent application. Thus the Mt. Baker Mining Co. agreed to sell to the plaintiffs this land within the Lulu Claim for $1. This mining deed was issued on July 10, 1903, in Portland, Ore., and conveyed an area 148 x 781 feet. With the matter closed, the patent land application proceeded.

Long Journey of the Ten Stamp Mill

From the time of discovery in 1897 to the summer of 1901, there had been many plans to begin construction on the ore mill, but none of these proposed plans was ever acted upon. In the summer of 1901, neither the ten-stamp mill nor any other ore-recovery equipment had been ordered or manufactured.

Then two events took place which set the wheels in motion: the first being the reorganization of the Lone Jack with new capital, and second the completion of the railroad to Maple Falls.

In July 1901, positive things began happening and longstanding plans finally fell in place. I.B. Hammond, president of the Hammond Manufacturing Co. of Portland, specializing in mining equipment, journeyed to Whatcom to meet with J.J. Donovan of the B.B. & B.C. Railroad to discuss arrangements for the transportation of equipment by rail to Maple Falls. The machinery included a ten stamp mill, a sawmill, a 4,000-foot tramway to transport ore from the mine to the stamp mill, and other related machinery.

There were major concerns about said machinery, most importantly

Mining equipment about to leave Maple Falls train station for the Lone Jack. (WWU-CPNEW)

being the mechanics of its delivery to the isolated mine and also the actual onsite construction. With the rail to Maple Falls, the section of wagon road from Sumas to Maple Falls had been eliminated and this was indeed an improvement to the transportation problem. The corduroy wagon road from Maple Falls to Shuksan had continued to be a real transportation issue, though the most pressing problem for transporting the equipment would be the trail from Shuksan to the mill site.

Can you imagine the shock and disappointment to Hammond when he arrived in Maple Falls in mid-summer to discover the wagon road leading up the North Fork was totally impassable? The road left Maple Falls and meandered through the giant fir and cedars. Up to this particular time, there hadn't been any heavy equipment taken beyond Maple Falls because there had been no one but settlers past that point.

Hammond returned to Sumas after several days of futile efforts at getting his supplies forwarded from Maple Falls to Shuksan. Hammond reported, surely with a broken spirit, that the first three miles of road out from Maple Falls were in horrible condition, and that it would be impossible for him to convey his heavy machinery to Shuksan unless the road received immediate attention from the county authorities.

Superintendent Stanislawsky arrived from the Mount Baker Mining District and began pressing the community to find a reasonably responsible party to establish a pack train from Maple Falls to the mines. At present, he said, the whole of the county's trade depended upon the actions of the owner of a half-dozen horses, a shyster who charged an exorbitant price for inferior service, and was wholly unable to perform half the packing that was now needed in the district. His company was ready to contract for several tons of freight,

Mining equipment in Shuksan heading for the Lone Jack. (WWU-CPNEW)

and other parties were also willing to contract for future service. From 50 to 100 tons needed to be packed this fall, and a good pack train of 25 animals, under charge of competent men, could reap a harvest on the trail. At this time a nine-horse pack train, operated by a man named Norman McDonald, was operating to Shuksan from Maple Falls and completed two trips a week.

County commissioner Kline returned from a trip six miles beyond Maple Falls, where he'd traveled to inspect the road leading to Shuksan. Contractors were at that time working on the road to make it suitable for freighting. Hammond expected to have 30 horses at Maple Falls within a night when the work of trafficking their ore-recovery machinery would commence. The ten stamp mill was expected to arrive in Maple Falls within 10 days. Stanislawsky, arriving in Maple Falls with a number of big horse teams with wagons, at once began loading goods from the railcars for the Post-Lambert.

On Nov. 5, 1901, Stanislawsky reported that Smith completed freighting 35,000 to 70,000 pounds from Maple Falls to Shuksan, which included the sawmill, the tramway cable, pipe ranging in size from 8 to 20 inches, and other equipment. The first attempt to transport the stamp mill mortars from Maple Falls to Shuksan failed on account of their heavy weight and thus forced the decision to change from a wagon to sled. The mortars for the stamp mills were the cast-iron bases used for each of the five stamp mills. The mortar bases were the heaviest items of all of the equipment and there was no way to disassemble them into lighter/smaller pieces.

On Feb. 1, 1902, F. Powell, the engineer for the Hammond Manufacturing Co. who was providing all the machinery, had traveled to Whatcom for a meeting with Stanislawsky to discuss the problems they were having regarding transporting all the machinery to the site. It was the intention of the Hammond Co. to move the machinery over the range while there was still a firm crust on the snow. George Smith of Sumas had the contract to transport the big mortar bases. The massive parts of the mill would be carried over to the mill site as rapidly as the weather would permit.

The whole of the machinery, they decided, would be loaded on 13 custom-made sleds and these would be pulled over the range by a 15-horse-power steam donkey engine. The engine would be anchored to a large selected tree and the loads pulled to it. Then the donkey engine, which was similarly mounted on a sled, would disconnect from the loads, moving the cables to a point further up the route, and pull itself to that point. After anchoring itself to another large tree, the men reconnected the engine to the loads and pulled them forward. This operation was repeated until the engine and machinery arrived at their destination. Stanislawsky stated that if present plans to move the stamps went according to plan, they would surely be dropped off at the Post-Lambert Mine site by that coming summer.

Thirteen sleds were custom built to haul freight to the Lone Jack. (WWU-CPNWS)

By the first of May, which was the intended time for moving over the snow at Twin Lakes Pass, the movement of the machinery was continuous but at a pace considerably slower than anticipated. This was partly because the path, intended only for horse-traffic, lay half as wide as needed for the donkey machine and sled. Furthermore, the route of traffic for the donkey and sleds was a straight line and the trail, with all of its inclines and turns, was not suitable. The trail, in most cases, ran high up on the steep hillside while the only suitable path for the moving of equipment was right up the creek bottom.

At this time, some of the machinery and supplies were still waiting to be moved from Maple Falls, yet the Portland office informed the Maple Falls Leader and the Sumas News that the stamp mill would be operable by the Fourth of July. The Mt. Baker Mining Co., like the others in the entire new district, was in a race to produce ore and extract gold. The shareholders of the Mt. Baker Mining Co. had surely been disappointed when The Great Excelsior Mill started milling gold on Aug. 28, 1902, even while the claim was discovered in August 1900—three years later than the Lone Jack. The Mt. Baker Mining Co. had boasted early on that it would be the first and most successful, yet while it was still moving equipment, the Excelsior was gaining fame. The Great Excelsior Mine was located across from the ongoing construction of the Nooksack Power Plant, below the Nooksack Falls.

A story in *The Daily Reveille* dated July 2, 1902, stated that now a new company, Nelson and Hall, was attempting to transport the first mortar from Shuksan to the mine on a specially constructed sled. The writer reported that the mortars were top-heavy and could cause the sled to overturn.

The trail to the Lone Jack passed another mine claim named the Britton Property and at this location on the trail the moving of the Lone Jack freight completely blocked traffic. Another company was having a problem getting past the blockage and requested of the Hammond Group that they build a way around.

By July 30, the moving of the freight was a total of three miles up Swamp Creek and approached the base of Swamp Creek/Twin Lakes Pass hill. By the end of September, all of the machinery and supplies were at a high point 300 to 400 feet higher than Twin Lakes on the ridge leading to the summit of Bear Mountain.

At this point, one could look directly down Lulu Gulch to the mill site. Here on the edge of a face, the workers anchored the steam donkey and lowered the sleds 4,000 feet down sheer cliffs. Near the top of Bear Mountain, there wasn't any running water and so water was carried from the lakes to the machine. Firewood was also very scarce at this elevation. Yet finally, after almost two years from Shuksan to here, they could see their destination.

Today one can only imagine the hardship, the cold and wet misery these men endured. History doesn't indicate that there was any loss of life in this two-year moving operation.

After all that effort and five years of work, Stanislawsky left the company and became involved with the Mt. Baker and Yale Mining Co. located along the Chilliwack River in Canada.

Finally on Oct. 21, 1902, it was reported that all of the machinery was at the mill site and the small and tireless steam donkey had been taken up to the mine, where it would be used in the installation of the cable for the tramway. The main track cable for the tram was one inch in diameter for downhill and 7/8 inch for the return. The traction cable was 5/8 inches in diameter, and had a one-direction length of 4,000 feet.

The sawmill had been in operation for a period of time cutting lumber from the nearby stands of timber. The sawmill was powered from a steam motor which received steam from a wood fired boiler, which would later provide the power to operate the mill. The mill's lumber was being used as quickly as it was produced in the construction of buildings, ore hoppers, and tram towers.

On Dec. 6, 1902, all the major machinery in the mill and the completed tram had been installed. The amount of work accomplished this year was totally unbelievable yet finally, after five years of time and an expenditure of a large sum of money ($40,000) the operation found itself prepared to produce gold. Andrew Ecklund, the foreman in charge of the mining operation, who was out for the holidays, had, at that time, blocked out in the mine over two million worth of $40 gold ore.

Post-Lambert officials told the *The Daily Reveille: "On June l3, 1903 that they secured the services of Samuel Gilmore, who for five years was employed as the amalgamator for the Treadwell Mine in Alaska, to take charge of its ten stamp mill."* Gilmore had traveled up to the mine and had stated that he believed the stamps would be dropping on or before July 1.

By July 28, 1903, the mill was operating on a limited basis with needed adjustments being made, and the main problem was the constant need to remove slack in the tramway cables. On Aug. 3, I.B. Hammond, of the Hammond Manufacturing Co. of Portland, passed through the city on his way to Portland from the Mount Baker Mining District, namely the Post-Lambert. Hammond's company had the contract for the installation of a ten-stamp mill and all other related machinery at the Lone Jack. It had been a tremendous task to get the machinery to the property and placing it in operation, an effort which had taken two years to accomplish, but it had been done.

Great credit was due to Hammond for bringing an undertaking so stupendous and fought with so many difficulties to a successful termination. The heavy machinery, weighing many tons, had to be transported over steep mountains to the mine. The company had expected aid from the county in the building of a road into the property, but this was never secured, and the company had to spend $4,500 in the construction of the road over which the mill and other machinery could be carried. The machinery was eventually taken through some of the roughest mountain country in the west without serious mishap.

The Lone Jack Mill was first set in stop and go motion on July 22, then put in constant operation a few days later. By the following summer, it was handling about 35 tons of ore per day. The ore was of a very high grade; large quantities had been stored ready for milling, and the future of the Post-Lambert looked bright. In the opinion of every mining expert who had ever visited the property, it was destined to become one of the greatest producers of wealth in the country.

Chapter 5

Lone Jack Gold

Mt. Baker Mining Co. Yearly Report for the Year of 1902

Following is the 1902 year-end report of the Mt. Baker Mining Co. and is issued to all shareholders by Mr. Henry Hahn, company president:

"The year of 1902 is the most successful year in the history of Mt. Baker Mining Co. to date with enormous success in preparing to finally proceed with an operating facility. In 1903, a few minor items remain to be installed, test runs made, adjustments needed and then hopefully the operation will produce gold by June 1903. Attached find a complete review of the total facility by the engineering firm of Oregon Mining Engineers of Portland. This firm was requested by the company's Portland office to report to all of the shareholders a factual report and also by doing so discharge any hesitancy from all past information."

1. Transportation to the Operation—The condition of the roads and trails system is only slightly improved from the time of discovery. However, the writer had no knowledge of the earlier conditions nor had visited the site previously. In 1897 at the discovery, the required travel time from Sumas to the Lone Jack was four days, and presently it is a three-day trip. The train trip to Maple Falls with a stage ride to Loop's Inn is made the first day, and a long horseback trip to the town of Shuksan is made the second day. The third day is a horseback trip up the Swamp Creek drainage to Twin Lakes Pass and thus around the shoulder of Bear Mountain to the Jack.

With the opening of the B.B. & B.C. Railroad Bellingham to Maple Falls, the first leg of the trip is greatly improved. The route from Maple Falls to the small growing community of Glacier is presently a reasonable wagon road. The route beyond Glacier to Shuksan, in the dry time of year (about three months out of the year), is a reasonable wagon road. The remainder of the year it is only suitable for long-legged horses and mules. All the major dangerous water crossings currently have been bridged with suitable structures.

The trail up Swamp Creek and over Twin Lakes Pass is in reasonable condition with yearly improvements completed and yearly maintenance being performed. The Mt. Baker Mining Co. is currently paying 50 to 60 percent of the Swamp Creek Trail expenses, which is being used by many other mining operations.

The Silesia Creek Trail, which starts at the U.S./Canada border and travels to the mill site, is in suitable shape because it doesn't cross any high mountain passes and is situated on the dry side of the mountain. This trail climbs 700 feet above Silesia Creek and then down to the mill site.

At the Twin Lakes Pass, the High Trail contours south at an almost-level grade to above Lulu Gulch and then switchbacks down to provide access to the Lulu workings. This High Trail is used mainly as a short-cut trail in returning packhorses to Twin Lakes. The Twin Lakes Pass Trail continues to the south and intersects the Silesia Creek Trail about one-quarter of a mile before crossing the Lulu Gulch. A new trail, which is named the Mill to Mine, was constructed this last year connecting the two up the Garrison Creek Ridge.

All named trails are in good condition. All named trails are suitable for winter use with proper tree blazing to identify the trail below.

Typical trail system near Twin Lakes. (J. Munroe)

Log bridge across Silesia Creek near Canadian border. (J. Munroe)

2. Mining—The mining operation at the Lone Jack is advanced ahead of the milling operation. The preliminary exploration started in 1898 and a complete mining operation has been carried on to date. At the discovery location, at an elevation of 5,360 feet, the gold-bearing quartz vein is completely visible on the surface, which allows the vein to be easily traced and direction determined. The discovery point is on a rock face that is yearly swept clean by avalanches of snow and other material. This rock face is approximately a 60 to 70 degree slope and, because of the above-named difficulties, the Lone Jack should at no time be mined from the point of discovery.

From an elevation of 5,300 feet, a level platform was blasted out of the rock face and a level 410-foot

Typical roadbed—Maple Falls. (WWU-CPNWS)

59

Haulageway adit—the Lone Jack with John Bullene. (M. Impero)

haulageway (adit) was driven in a westerly direction into Bear Mountain. The location of the haulageway is an improvement to the discovery point because of its location around and under the ridge crest thus being safer from avalanches. This site is an improvement, but it is still in a dangerous area. At a point 292 feet from the haulageway portal, a 60-degree ore drop raises to a sublevel 67 feet above the haulageway. This sublevel extends 80 feet NNW and 255 feet SSE from the top of the ore drop.

From the sublevel, six ore drops (passages) of approximately 40 degrees climb up a short distance to the Lone Jack stope (mining area). As the ore is removed out of the stope, it drops down one of the six ore chutes,

then is hauled down the sublevel in rail ore carts and deposited down the 60-degree ore drop (raise) to the haulageway. The ore is transported by ore cart out to the portal where the tramway upper ore hopper is located and dumped.

The entire mining operation above has been completely developed, and has a satisfactory working flow as of

Headwork construction—upper tramway. (WWU-CPNWS)

60

this writing. The 67-foot, 60-degree ore drop (raise) was constructed of sufficient size that a bulkhead of heavy-weight timbers was used to create an ore drop and manway. The manway is equipped with a permanent wood ladder and provided worker access from the portal to the stope. The ore drop is regulated at the bottom with a wood and steel ore flow gate. The sublevel is equipped with trackage and ore carts as is the lower haulageway tunnel. Trackage will be added to the stope area when the area is opened up in the future.

All the work areas are ventilated by gas-powered fan units. There are approximately 20 miners working at the mining work area. The stope (the mining area) work area has only a height of 30 to 36 inches, minimizing the need for handling waste rock. There is no compressed air at the works, but the installation of a future air compressor and air drilling equipment is expected to be initiated soon.

The drilling is being performed by the single or double-jack method. In the single-jack method, one man holds the drill in one hand and strikes the drill with a sledgehammer with his other arm. The double-jack method requires two men with one holding and rotating the drill and the second man swinging the sledgehammer.

Another development is that of the creation of a new carbide lamp which is to be fastened to the miner's helmet, replacing the troublesome candle. This new creation of the carbide

headlamp is found to be safer and more dependable. The headlamp uses only 9 percent the amount of oxygen from the air as compared to a miner candle and only 12 percent as much carbon dioxide is released back in the air compared to the candle. The improved fueled lamp operated for the total duration of a man shift.

Vertical ore drop. (J. Christenson)

Incline ore drop. (J. Christenson)

Inside stope area—rock pillar. (J. Christenson)

Inside with timber pillars. (J. Christenson)

Sloping stope area. (J. Christenson)

Stope with ghost dog. (J. Christenson)

63

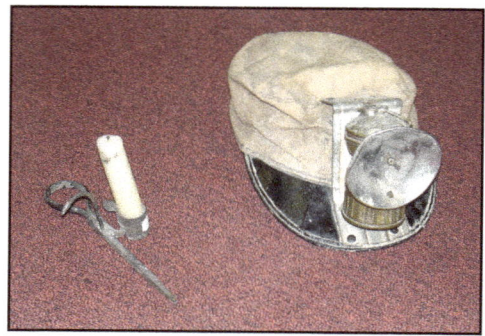

Miner candle and miner carbide lantern.
(M. Impero)

The workers' living quarters are located at the adit entry in a building which has served as a blacksmith shop, cookhouse, and bunkhouse for 3½ years. Workers requested to locate down to the highly improved living quarters at the mill site. Andy Ecklund, who has been at the Lone Jack from the beginning, is currently and has been from the beginning the superintendent at the mine.

Tramway bucket similar to Lone Jack.
(M. Impero)

The mining operation is expected to shut down in mid-January 1902, due to the fact that all available storage space is consumed. The west

Garrison Creek hillside. (M. Impero)

end of the haulageway and a portion of the sublevel are currently full of ore that is ready to mill. Because of extremely steep ground, there is no available storage space outside of the haulageway tunnel.

3. Tramway—The main track (riding) cables of the tramway are 1-inch diameter steel for the down direction and 7/8-inch diameter for the return in a length of approx. 4,000 feet each with an elevation difference from the mine to mill of 1,752 feet. Anchorage is provided for the track cable at the top of the tram by heavy-duty rock anchors and at the bottom by anchor cables that pass adjacent to the mill building and are connected to a series of large fir trees.

The lower end of the main track cable requires two turnbuckles—1¼ inches diameter x 4 feet long—along with the main counterweight device used to tighten any slack that may occur to the cable. These two main track cables are separate and are not connected in any way, however they are parallel and uniformly spaced. The second cable is the 5/8-inch diameter traction (pulling and lowering) cable and is provided in one continuous length. The traction cable passes around the head works and around the tail works.

The head works and tail works consist of a 6-foot diameter bullwheel, which changes the direction of the ore buckets. The traction cable also has a tightening device, which is part of the tail bullwheel system.

The buckets are connected to the traction cable by means of a clamping device and ride on the track cable with a system of two sheaves each. There are 34 buckets on the tramway at one time, with 17 traveling down full and 17 returning back empty. These buckets must maintain their spacing, which is vital for a smooth and balanced operation. Each bucket has a capacity of 500 pounds of ore.

The tramway support towers are ideally spaced approximately 150 yards to 200 yards apart and approximately 30 feet above the ground to be above heavy winter snowfalls. When the tramway crossed Garrison Gulch, the towers are about 200 yards apart and at one point the cables are between 200 and 300 feet above the ground.

The travel speed and stopping the total system is controlled by a manual brake on the headwork bull wheel. A worker is stationed on the ridge crest above Garrison Creek, below the mine adit, and acts as the signalman for the operation of the tram with the use of the electric telephone. The tram towers are of a four-leg design and constructed to a double-strength standard with heavy cable guys to safely protect against potential avalanche damage.

The buckets are disconnected from the cable by releasing the clamp at the top station and bottom station. The buckets then ride on a circular steel track that allows the bucket to be loaded at the top and unloaded at the bottom. The buckets, when ready to continue, are re-clamped to the traction cable. The system is totally powered by gravity and requires no cost to provide the power.

The tramway will be used to haul material and supplies between the mine and mill. However, the system must be kept in balance by the proper bucket spacing. The tramway is not recommended for the movement of workers between the mill and mine due to the dangerous height in crossing Garrison Gulch.

The buckets at the headwheel will be loaded from a steel-lined wood ore hopper and a slide gate located in the bottom controls the flow. Similarly, the ore is dumped at the bottom into a steel-lined hopper and is directed to the mill. The tramway will be operated in day-light hours only.

4. Mill—The ore mill building location is at an elevation of approximately 3,600 feet and approximately 850 feet above Silesia Creek. The hillside is extremely steep and the mill is located on a sloping benched area. The site is on the south side of the avalanche chute that continues down from the crest of Bear Mountain all the way to Silesia Creek. This avalanche gulch is named Lulu Gulch.

The mill building is safely located 75 feet into the old-growth fir timber. The mill building is a typical layout using the steep hillside that creates the flow of the gold ore from the upper level to the waste pile. The gold ore from the mine via the tramway enters the mill building on the high side and is deposited within the ore storage bin. The ore travels down a chute to the grizzly, whereupon any ore 1 inch or less passes through to the feeder. The grizzly is a steel panel (10 feet x 7 feet) made from steel bars spaced 2 inches apart. The ore that cannot pass the grizzly bar spacing then continues down to the Blake Ore Breaker Model No. 2 (1 inch x 7 inches) to be crushed down to a 1-inch minimum and then returns to the feeder.

The 1-inch minimum ore is fed by the Challenge Ore Feeder to both stamp mills, where the final crushing takes place. The mill has two Fraser & Chalmers Stamp Mill Machines, which contains five 850 pound stamps, each with a mortar base weight of 5,000 pounds. The stamp mill has a mortar base, which is made of cast iron (the heaviest weight in the whole operation) and each stamp has a shaft with a heavy weight on the bottom which is mechanically raised and dropped in the proper order on the gold bearing ore. Each stamp drops at the rate of 90 times per minute and the recommended order of dropping is 2, 4, 1, 5, and 3.

The ore is pulverized in the mortar base to a very fine powder-like material and a moderate volume of water is added to convert the ore into slurry. In this fine crushing operation, the gold is separated from the other particles within the ore. The stamp mill base, which is again called the mortar, is closed on three sides with the downhill side open. This opening has a fine mesh screen of number 100 size. At the point that ore is crushed fine, it will now pass through the fine screen. The screen is a copper screen and is coated with a fine layer of mercury. Also, on the other interior sides of the mortar base are copper plates that are covered with mercury. These three plates and the screen are removed when the stamp mill is taken out of operation for cleanup.

When the slurry is free to pass the stamp mill, it flows out upon the amalgamating table (5 feet x 10 feet). These two tables are directly in line below the mill and are built at a slight slope downhill. The table is constructed of wood supports and a wood top. The wood top is then covered with a sheet of copper, which is then coated with a fine film of mercury such as what was applied to the copper sheets and screen in the stamp mill. This copper plate with mercury is the second of three gold recovery systems used and the third is the use of a concentration table.

The concentration table is also a sloping table, which the slurry now travels upon. The table is sloping in two directions and has a smooth surface with 1/8 inch-high ribs across the surface. The table has a mechanical vibration system and also has a supply of fresh water running across the surface to wash away the lighter, non-gold materials. At this point, the remaining slurry passes beyond the mine building and is considered waste.

This mill operation is expected to operate with a three-man crew working 10 hours per day for

two shifts. The mill was designed for continuous operation with maintenance being done on the machinery while in operation. As with the stamp mill, one or more stamps can be taken out of service for maintenance and the remaining stamps can function as normal.

The mill is designed for a gold recovery cleanup and this recovery is expected to be done every three to four weeks. At cleanup, the concentration table is carefully cleaned with gold being found above the table ribs. Now the copper plates, which is where the bulk of the gold is recovered, are completely cleaned by scraping and brushing to save all of the mercury that now contains the free gold attracted to the mercury. The mercury and gold mixture is handled with extreme care, using a special container.

On the lower backside of the mill building, is a small lean-to room approximately 14 feet by 16 feet, which is very well sealed and is separated from the rest of the building with a locked exterior entrance only. This area is designed as the assay office and mercury/gold separation room. One man who serves as the assayer also serves as the man responsible for the mercury/gold separation. The mercury/gold mixture, after being carefully moved to this room, is placed in a gold retort Model No. 7 and high heat is placed at the bottom. The retort top must be securely sealed with the vent pipe running in a loop and placed into a vat of water. As the heat is increased, the mercury vaporizes, flowing into the cold water and forming back to a solid in the bottom of the water vat. A responsible and trained worker must perform this process because of the high health danger due to the possible vapor leaks and the value of the recovered gold.

After the removal of all of the mercury, the gold is in a liquid state and is poured into ingot molds. In a free milling ore such as the Lone Jack, one-sixth ounce of mercury per ton of ore milled would be the usual loss that might be expected. With ordinary ore, the amalgamation should be retorted once in every 21 to 30 days, also named the cleanup, returning the mercury for use in batteries again, minus above loss. The Lone Jack stamp mill will lose mercury at the rate of 1/6 to 1/3 ounce per ton or about 12 to 15 pounds per month.

The building is constructed in four levels, each being used in the procedure of processing of the ore. The building is constructed of Alaska cedar being used as beams, columns, and lumber that is being cut from the abundant surrounding trees. Cedar shakes for the roof area are also cut from area cedar trees. The size of the building is approximately 30 feet by 60 feet.

The above mill operation will require 30 horsepower to operate and handle approximately 15 to 18 tons of ore per 24-hour day. The water requirement of the operation of the system is 72 gallons per hour per stamp, and 60 gallons per hour per

Lone Jack Stamp Mill near completion 1902. (WWU-CPNWS)

Completed Lone Jack Stamp Mill 1903. (Chechaco and Sourdough)

Lone Jack Stamp Mill in winter. (Chechaco and Sourdough)

TYPICAL AMALGAMATION/CONCENTRATION MILL

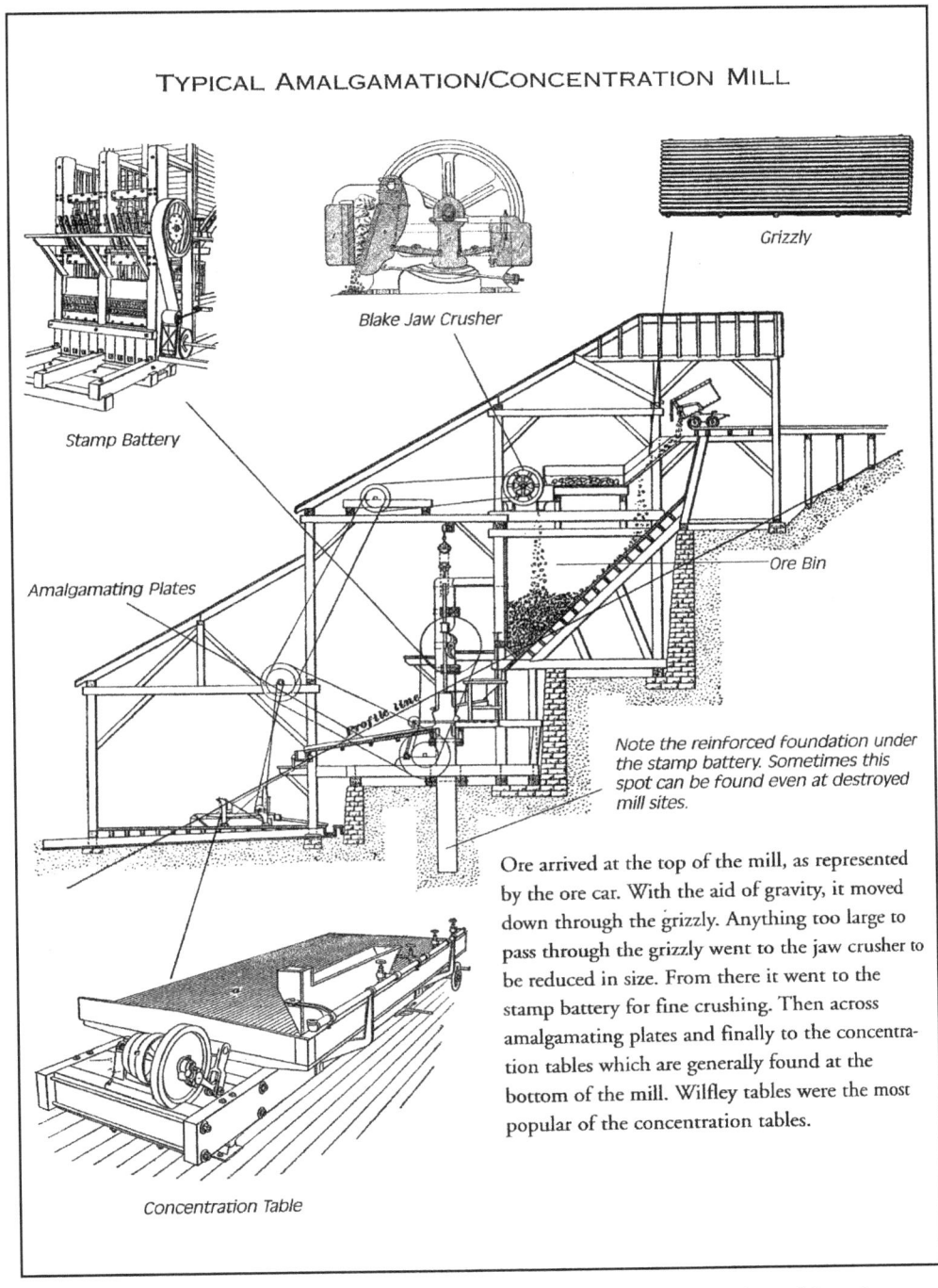

Grizzly

Blake Jaw Crusher

Stamp Battery

Amalgamating Plates

Ore Bin

Note the reinforced foundation under the stamp battery. Sometimes this spot can be found even at destroyed mill sites.

Ore arrived at the top of the mill, as represented by the ore car. With the aid of gravity, it moved down through the grizzly. Anything too large to pass through the grizzly went to the jaw crusher to be reduced in size. From there it went to the stamp battery for fine crushing. Then across amalgamating plates and finally to the concentration tables which are generally found at the bottom of the mill. Wilfley tables were the most popular of the concentration tables.

Concentration Table

Cross section of how the Lone Jack Stamp Mill would have looked. The Jack would not have had the ore cart dumping at the top level because the Jack ore was delivered by cable tramway.

PLATE 36.

STAMP BATTERY.
TEN STAMPS

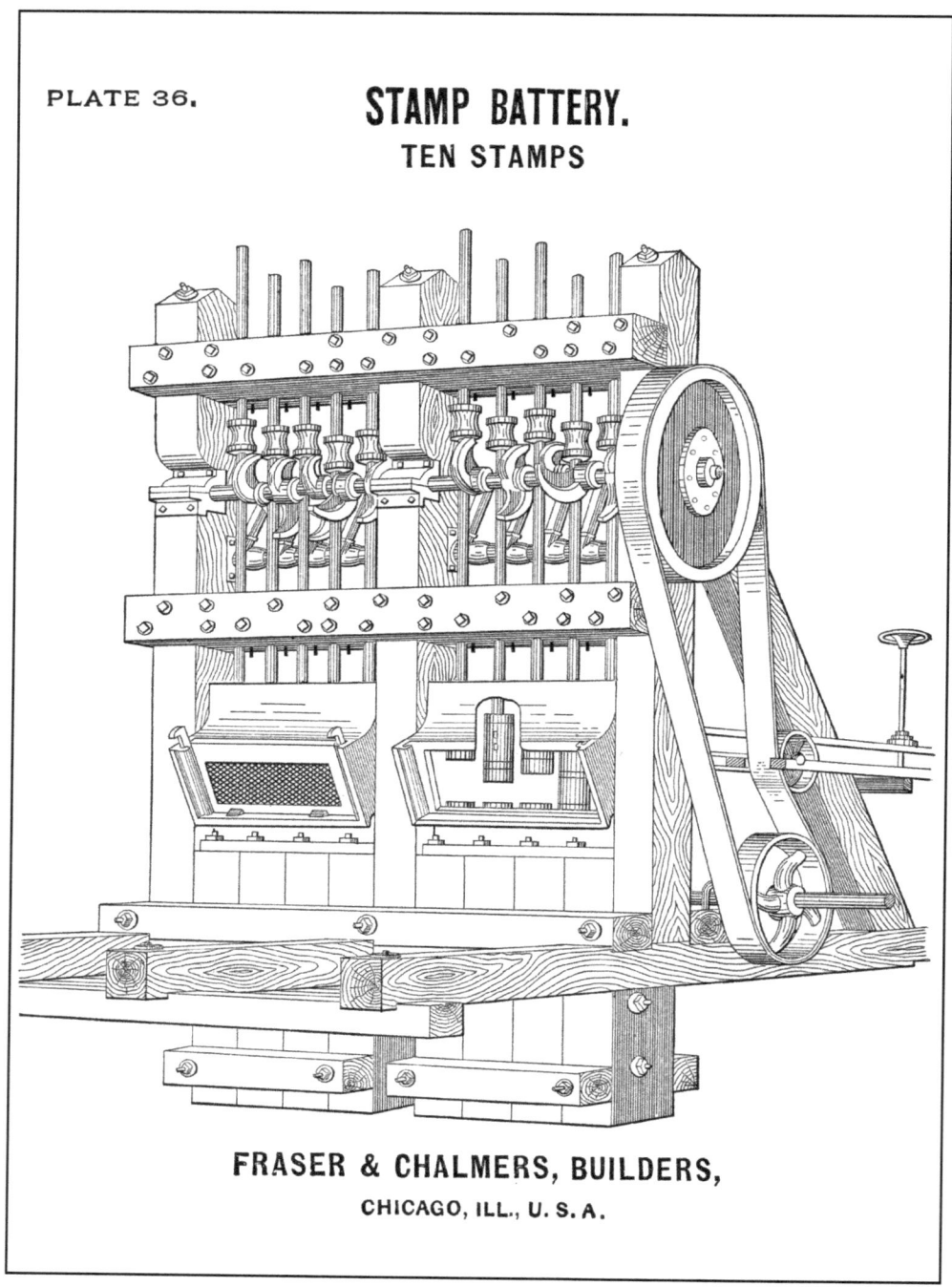

FRASER & CHALMERS, BUILDERS,
CHICAGO, ILL., U. S. A.

The stamp mills at the Jack were similar to these Fraser & Chalmers Model H.
However the stamps at the Jack were made completely of steel and cast iron. (F. Stahlbush)

Five stamp mill made completely from steel and iron with stamp shoe sitting to the left of the mill located at the Winthrop Museum. (G. Byeman)

Five stamp mill with discharge opening. (G. Byeman)

Stamp mill after the 1907 fire—one stamp mill is in a vertical position however the second had fallen over. (J. Munroe)

Picture shows the stamp mill in position, 1940. (UW)

Stamp mill after the 1907 fire. Picture taken Sept. 20, 1922. (J. Munroe)

Picture shows both mills in a fallen state, 2006. (G. Byeman)

72

each settler. The mill and mine are connected by a telephone system with three stations: the top at the loading station, at the point where the tramway breaks over the ridge, and one at the mill. The telephone wire is connected to the tramway tower thus making it easy to inspect. This telephone system is used in the operation of the tram, and general communication between the mill and mine.

5. Support Equipment—With the completion of the mill building, all of the operating equipment is established in permanent place. This equipment provides power, water, lights, and heat. An Impulse Pelton Water Wheel provides the electrical power needs of the total mill and the water source comes to the wheel by

a steel pipe pinstock with 500-foot water pressure from a point above on Garrison Creek. This intake was reasonably low enough down the hill that the possibility of freezing in the dead of winter was slight. An improved screening system must be added with maintenance to insure a constant power source. This Pelton Wheel is located under a lean-to roof on the south side and drives a small Westinghouse (60 cycle) Generator off a series of belts. The generator provides electrical needs for lighting the mill building, bunkhouse building, and to operate the telephone system.

The Pelton Wheel is an excellent choice of power because of the lack of maintenance and basically required no other source of energy such as

Steam plant that provides the steam to operate the steam motor. However this plant also heated the water to allow year-round operation. (G. Byeman)

Two cylinder steam motor. (G. Byeman)

wood, oil, or coal. A flume provides a second source of water that is an open ditch which runs south of the mill and intersects a stream that comes off the south end of Bear Mountain. The water travels in the ditch to the mine and is stored in a wood tank. This tank provides water to run the mill and water for the bunk/cook house. It may be expected that at the coldest point of winter that the flume (ditch) may freeze solid which would cause the whole operation to shut down.

The main power source that provides the power to operate all of the equipment in the ore mill is a two-cylinder steam motor. This steam motor is the essential piece of equipment and if this were to go down, the whole mill operation would cease. The mounting of this motor is a simple application, and from an engineering viewpoint we recommend

a backup motor. The boiler at the mill site is an item that has two uses; the first being the power source for the above named steam motor, and secondly to be used as a hot water heater for the operation of the mill. To operate the mill one must have a year-round supply of water and with the extreme cold weather of the winter in the Cascade Mountains the boiler is used to preheat the water to operate the ore mill.

The sawmill is an "American" with a capacity of between 4,000 to 5,000 board feet per day. This mill is powered by the steam motor with the boiler. The sawmill is located in a position directly above the steam motor and wood-fired boiler. This mill was used to saw lumber for the upper headwork, tramway, mill building, bunkhouse, and timber needed within the mine workings. All the above are in good repair, however the sawmill shows wear.

6. Gold Safeguarding & Transportation—With the upcoming operation of the mill and cleanup of the gold, the question of safeguarding and shipping the gold out to a Whatcom bank is a question of utmost importance. As the mill operates, there is constantly a supply of newly found gold at the base of the stamp mill, the amalgamation table, and the concentration table. As the cleanup date nears, the amount increases and this area must be kept at a high level of security. No one other than the stamp mill superintendent or only the most trusted employee should be allowed in the lower deck of the mill. At a point as the cleanup is approaching, a night watchman is recommended. No unknown visitor should be allowed to remain in the camp for any period of time.

Any person that can get his hands on a quantity of amalgamated mix (gold and mercury mix) can develop a method of removing the gold. A method that has recently surfaced is to take a large potato, cut it in half, hollow out a pocket, and place an amount of the mix in the hollow. Next, wire it shut and place in a campfire to cook. After a period of time, remove the potato from the fire. As the potato cooks, the heat vaporizes the mercury and the vapors are dissipated into the potato. Upon opening the potato, one can find a solid bead of gold. This potato method and many others have been used to extract the gold from an amalgamated mix by a thief.

In the assay office and gold recovery room, there is a safe that is securely anchored to a concrete base. We feel that the best way to move the gold is that it be carried by one of the company's most trusted employees, a person with a real feel for wilderness travel and a feel for possible attack. The reason for the gold being carried by man is that this has to be done year-round, making the travel by horse in the winter snows impossible. Also, if the carrier were attacked on horseback with the conditions of the trail, an escape by horse would be impossible.

The normal way for carrying the gold is a short lightweight coat that can be worn under a normal coat with pockets for the gold bars. The shape of the proposed gold casting ingot is fashioned with this in mind. The gold should be transported as soon as possible after cleanup in reasonable weather but in no case should this movement be on a scheduled basis. The carrier should be armed and have at least one guard traveling with him.

A favorable thing about the Lone Jack operation is that the gold can be taken out in three directions; two being by a U.S. route and the third by the Canada route, and in no way should there be any pattern to the upcoming trip. No one other than the carrier and the trusted guard should know the time and the route. A shipping paper upon leaving the mill should be signed by the mill superintendent and a signed receipt obtained at the bank upon arrival.

7. Workers Facilities—The first thing that was constructed at the mill site was the bunk house for all of the workers at the mine and the mill. This building (24 feet by 34 feet) was built about 75 feet south of the mill building and is located in old-growth timber. With the completion of the structure, all workers including the workers at the mine site are now being housed and fed at the mill site. The building at the mine portal will be continued to be used as the upper blacksmith shop and storage. The bunkhouse building is a two-story structure with an interior stairway. A room off the side of the building is used as a laundry, clothes hanging area, and storage for dry goods. The main floor is a commons area, with bunks along the back wall for 12 men. On the second floor is the main bunk house area with sleeping quarters for 18 men. This facility is equipped with two wood heaters.

The cookhouse building is a combination cooking and dining facility with all the most modern equipment. The meat cooler building, near the rear entrance, is eight feet square and is cooled by running water on the roof. A Chinese man is the cook and his Indian wife is the general flunkie for the whole building. This is a well-lit building with windows on all walls and the second floor ends. Keeping a well-rounded supply of food and supplies for the winter time operation is necessary because through the winter months there will be no freight coming in. This building will need to function as the commissary store for the workers and sell items such as gloves, boots, coats, socks, and tobacco. Under no circumstances should any form of alcohol be at the operation. This facility is average in grade and quality within the mining standards.

Cook/bunk house which survived the 1907 fire and was standing in 1922. (J. Munroe)

We thank the management of the Mt. Baker Mining Co. in selecting us to submit this report. If any shareholder has any question concerning the report, please direct such questions to the company secretary and these questions will be forwarded to our firm for answering.

Oregon Mining Engineers
Portland, Oregon

Currently the total expenditures for the construction and equipping the operation have exceeded $45,000 with all of these debts having been paid off. The Post-Lambert Mine (Lone Jack) is owned and operated by the Mt. Baker Mining Co. with capital stock of $100,000.

We thank you for your patience in getting to this point and stand ready to be processing gold in 1903.

Respectfully Submitted,

MT. BAKER MINING CO.
HAHN & FRIEDE

Lone Jack Gold

The Blade in New Whatcom, dated Wednesday, Aug. 26, 1903 under a heading titled "Industrial," presented the following story: "The Mount Baker Mining District is no longer a doubtful quantity. A cleanup has been made and the gold is on its way out. The result is beyond man's wildest dreams, and makes former tales from the camp look like thirty cents.

"H. Wright of Tyler & Wright of this city arrived in town last evening from the Mt. Baker country the bearer of this startling information regarding the cleanup at the Post-Lambert mine. The mill had run 25 days. The net result is $27,000. Leo Friede, secretary of the company, was expected to arrive here yesterday, and will no doubt come out today with the gold.

"The mill is only a ten-stamp plant, but the ore is very high-grade. An average of 35 tons of rock per day has been treated since the mill started up in July. The ore has averaged better than $35 per ton. There is a large body blocked out ready for stoping, an ore reserve large enough it is said to last the mill a long time.

"This run indicates that the mine with its present equipment working on its present grade of ore can pay about $300,000 net annual profit. The result means that a great impetus will be given mining in the Mt. Baker District as it thoroughly makes the reputation the mines of this section."

In September 1903, the Blade reported: "The freight company Nestos and McDonald announced transporting to the Jack 55 tons of supplies for the approaching winter to allow the Company to operate year-round. Using two four-horse teams with wagons, and seventeen-pack horses, the company is moving approximately 2,200 lbs. of freight per day.

"They also stated now that the mill and the mine are operating, all information regarding the operation is being highly guarded from the general public. The obvious reason is the safe-guarding of all information concerning gold shipments. The second cleanup was complete the second week of October with an amount less than the previous because the milling period of time was less than the first.

"With the continuous problems with the tram which allows only to transport a reduced amount of twenty tons of ore per day in lieu of the planned 35 tons per day. The Company stated that they plan to add ten additional stamps and a cyanide plant in the spring of 1904. Also reported that the mine foreman has finished intense work in mine development with five or six ore drops that conveys ore from the main ore stope to the haulage tunnel.

"In December, Andy Ecklund, who is always involved with one or two armed guards, transported to town the fourth cleanup from the Jack and the dollar amount is reported to be consistent with the others. Ecklund added that twice as many ore buckets have been installed thus the problem with the tramway has been solved. With 40 tons of ore per day moving down the hillside to the mill a monthly cleanup from this point forward is expected to average $42,000."

On Jan. 8, 1904, Big Andy, like clockwork, once more arrived in town with his guards with the January cleanup. In middle of spring, President Hahn reported that half of the 10-stamp mill (one five-stamp mill) was shut down because of the lack of adequate water to operate. Hahn also stated that all mining operations to date have been carried out from the Lone Jack, however the mining will also commence next year on the Lulu. The news that all shareholders have been waiting for was received from President Hahn with the announcement that the first dividend will be paid in the summer of 1904.

Big Andy

Andrew "Big Andy" Ecklund was born and raised in his homeland of Sweden, and as a young man struck out for a career as a sailor traveling around the world. On one trip up the Pacific Coast, his ship stopped in New Whatcom to take on a cargo of fir and cedar lumber and either Ecklund jumped ship or had made plans to settle in New Whatcom. With a large Scandinavian community at the Blue Canyon Coal Mine on the south end of Lake Whatcom, Ecklund easily settled in and found employment, being hired by Peter Larson.

Following his arrival, there were two mining accidents at the Blue Canyon. In the first, all 23 miners who were underground in the mine were killed with only the four workmen who were topside being spared. After a second accident, Ecklund determined that the time was right to leave the mine and he relocated to Whatcom, where he met, courted, and married Christine Helmgren. Ecklund's next employment for one season was at the Lake Whatcom Mill, which Peter Larson was also involved.

In 1898 there was an immediate need for experienced miners and the only skilled miners were those trained in the area of coal mines. With his experience at the Blue Mountain Coal Mine, the big Swede Andy was an obvious choice and so Big Andy joined with Henry Stanislawsky in the development work on the Lone Jack. The planned work consisted of preliminary work, trail work, and constructing the first buildings. Within a few months, Ecklund was assigned the position of an assistant to Stanislawsky.

With the mine sale to English and Son for $350,000, and Stanislawsky relieved of his position, Andrew Ecklund continued on in the position of mainly developing the mine site. With his wife and two children relocating to Whatcom in 1904, Ecklund resided at the Lone Jack for up to six months.

Ecklund, a man of extreme patience, became totally dedicated to the Lone Jack from the beginning. He remained all the way through the lack of funding, inability to move the equipment to the site, lawsuits, and of course the terrible winter conditions. With many other types of employment available at the time, Ecklund could have had various jobs that would have been a far easier life and allowed him to be with his growing family, but he elected to remain isolated at the Lone Jack.

On one of his trips out, Ecklund at the request of management traveled in to New Whatcom to meet a new camp cook and direct him to the Lone Jack. This unfamiliar cook had taken

the job at the Lone Jack and would be bringing along with his wife their 3-year-old son. At Shuksan, after parting company with the saddle and pack horses, all their belongings were to be carried up the Swamp Creek Trail to Twin Lakes, then to the stamp mill on their backs.

The small boy presented a problem since he wasn't able to travel on the steep, muddy, mountainous trail. Ecklund offered a solution. He placed the small-undersized boy in a gunnysack with his head out through the top of the sack, put him up, threw the sack over his shoulder and easily strolled the eight-mile trail back to the Jack.

In 1902 with the installation of the tramway complete, and with the equipment testing taking place, Big Andy at 5:00 one afternoon was completing his daily rounds of the operation. Upon doing so, he discovered some sheaves in the mill end that were making a grinding noise. After a closer inspection, his jacket sleeve was suddenly drawn into the traveling cable and his hand quickly went through the mechanism. Instantly the fingers on one hand were sheared off, with only the thumb remaining.

Ecklund succeeded in withdrawing his arm and, in seeing his mauled hand, his first thought was how to get medical treatment quickly. With no method to provide transportation for the injured man, his only option was to walk down to Glacier and take the train to the New Whatcom.

The injured hand, after being cleaned, was bandaged to prevent excessive bleeding. Accompanied by an escort, Big Andy set out on the strenuous journey of walking to Glacier, which also required travel throughout the night. In hearing of the accident, the B.B. & B.C. train was held at the Glacier Depot as directed by J.J. Donovan, superintendent of the railroad.

After being treated by Doctor Axtell in New Whatcom, Ecklund was transported to the local hospital for a recovery period lasting over a few weeks. The only positive matter gained by Ecklund is that the Mt. Baker Mining Co. increased his pay from $110 to $150 per month.

Cress Brothers

Within a week after the accident while Big Andy was recovering in a hospital bed, a 16-year-old young man by the name of John Cress from Colorado quietly approached him. Cress, from a family of miners, paid the visit to the patient to discuss the possibility of being hired at the Lone Jack. After listening to Cress, Ecklund determined that young Cress reminded him of himself in his youth seeking his first opportunity in America. Ecklund elected to hire the young, inexperienced man, but after his recent accident felt that the young man required a careful eye for his safety.

Along with another young new employee, Cress reported for employment at the Lone Jack as directed by Ecklund. The two walked in from Glacier and reported to Sam

Gilmore, general superintendent. They cut and dragged shoring posts to the ore mill on the snow all winter with all the work being performed by hand. These posts would be carried later by the tramway to the mine level.

Cress stated, "I was thus employed all winter with 10 feet of snow on the ground, and in rain or snow, without losing a day. Many times I wished I could get out of it all and go back to Colorado, where I had come from, but there was no chance. But when spring opened so beautifully, I thought better of my conditions and decided to stay, in fact really liked the layout and remained for seven years."

When Ecklund returned weeks later to his work at the mine, 16-year-old John Cress was the youngest hand in the camp. Ecklund took a liking to his young adopted protégé and acted as the boy's guardian-protector until he learned the rules and methods of the mine's operating force.

As he grew older and experienced, Cress advanced in responsibility and acted as watchman, packer, hunter, and guard at different times. In all of these available positions, Cress found his keenest pleasure in being the camp hunter for fresh meat.

In February 1906, David Cress, John's younger brother by two years, became employed at the Lone Jack. In winter months, all foot traffic to the operation traveled up the Chilliwack Trail through Canada. On such a trip, John Cress was returning to the mine with his newly hired brother.

As the two were approaching a roadhouse, where they intended to spend the night, John advised David that a German man named Hipkope, with his wife and eight pretty daughters, operated the house. He advised David not to make any off-color jokes to the girls because the father was extremely protective of them and with a remark the brothers could be sleeping in the barn.

He also told his brother that they could travel further up the trail to a second roadhouse but the owner of this roadhouse allowed his six to eight dogs to sleep on the guest beds. When the owner has guests, he boots the dogs out of the house and in this way the fleas are passed from dog to guest. Like good American boys, the two Cress brothers picked the roadhouse with the girls.

Both of the brothers, at different times, were sent into the surrounding mountains to hunt deer, bear and mountain goats for the company. Both of the Cress brothers were ready to meet the challenge of supplying fresh meat as it was more of a pleasure than a labor, even though it called for both ingenuity and endurance. Whoever shot a goat, bear or deer would receive two days of pay but received no pay if the hunting trip was unsuccessful. After a few years, both Dave and John gave up hunting because of the lack of success caused by the abundance of prospectors in the area.

With the problem of the lack of fresh meat, Dave Cress was dispatched to Glacier to drive back two living beef steers. When he returned the following day with those two steers in tow, the look on the 35 workers' faces was one of complete happiness.

When John Cress arrived, the Lone Jack was operating at full capacity with two shifts per day. His first position was that of catching the buckets at the mill station of the tramway, and operating the jaw crusher, grizzly, and feeder to the stamp mill.

Sam Gilmore occupied the lower end, which consisted of stamp mill, amalgamation table and concentration table. Sam's brother, Jack, replaced Sam at the lower end on the night shift. The buckets that rode on the track cable were lifted up by striking a heavy timber, which places the buckets on a half-round track that goes around outside the bottom head-wheel. Then the bucket clamp is released and the bucket stops over the ore bunker and is dumped. The buckets are then reconnected to the track cable for the return trip to the top. The noise within the mill building was unbearably loud with stamp mill and crusher operating, creating a sound similar of a passing train.

The amalgamation copper plates were located in the lower level in the mill building; this is where the actual gold accumulation took place. This location was restricted to all visitors and strictly enforced by the topside man, such as John Cress when Sam Gilmore wasn't present.

On one occasion, Mr. Hahn, president of the company, journeyed to the Lone Jack for an inspection. He entered the mill unannounced and continued down the stairs to the lower floor, where Gilmore was present. Dave Cress shouted to him above the sound of the equipment to stop, not knowing who he was, and would not allow him to pass. Gilmore, seeing what was going on, went to Hahn's rescue.

Gilmore and Hahn were extremely impressed with young Cress' attitude toward guarding of the lower floor. This guarded area, which included the amalgamation and concentration tables, is where the gold built up on the plates. By the time that monthly cleanup was performed, there could be a large build-up. There was no record at the Lone Jack of any worker helping himself to the gold and particularly in wintertime. If you got yourself fired for stealing, you would likely walk out by yourself.

The two Cress brothers were short, stocky young men of exceptional physical stamina. Dave stated more than once that the brothers could each carry in an 80-pound load from Glacier to the Lone Jack in 12 hours. Dave placed a new cook stove on his back for the trip from Glacier to the Lone Jack. However, when they then added a sack of flour in the oven, that proved to be beyond his limit.

Near Disasters

Mercury or quicksilver, which it was called at that time, proved to be the cause of two near-disasters for Dave Cress while he was operating the jaw crusher. On one hot summer afternoon, a mason jar of clear liquid was noticed by him. It was setting on the bottom step of the stairs leading down to the stamp mill floor. With occasional glances at what he thought to be a jar of good old mountain drinking water, the more thirsty he became.

When the crusher was taken off line momentarily, Cress decided to dash down and grab a swallow. The moment that the "water" struck his mouth, he recognized immediately by the odor that it was mercury, not water. Quickly spitting it out, Cress ran to an open-running water pipe and rinsed his mouth the best he could.

This jar of mercury was used to add a few drops directly to the stamp mill in the gold recovery system. With no after-effects from his little drink, Cress disclosed the incident to no one.

Later the same summer following a cleanup, Cress heard a man yelling down in the assay/gold recovery room. Upon entering, he discovered the room was full of mercury vapor. The man in charge of the room where the separation of the gold from the mercury took place had failed to secure the lid on the retort cooker and vapor escaped into the atmosphere.

He yelled at Cress to hold down the lid so that he could replace and drive in the wedge that held the lid. With the lid secured, he yelled at Dave to get the hell out. Cress lost some of his hair, which grew back in a short period, and he also lost some of his teeth at a young age. The man who remained working among the fumes had serious health problems within a few years. In later years at the Lone Jack, Dave Cress became the man that extracted the gold from the mercury.

Working at the Jack

Dave and John Cress became completely fed up with the attitude of Sam Gilmore, who operated the mill. The tram traveled down the mountainside under the weight of loaded ore buckets and returned empty buckets to the top. This one particular day, having reached the point of not caring if they both were fired, the brothers decided to overload the returning buckets with mine shoring posts. After placing a large quantity of posts on the tram, it stopped traveling and would not continue up or down.

Gilmore then fired them both; however, he rehired them the next day. The only method to solve the tram problem was to place a heavy pipe inside the spokes of the headwheel, then to turn the headwheel by hand moving the cable two feet at a time. It required the remaining part of the day for the tram to start flowing again.

With Gilmore being extremely moody, Dave Cress continually requested of Big Andy Ecklund that he be employed at the mine rather than the mill. The top end of the mine site employed approximately 25 to 30 miners. After being persistent with Ecklund, Dave Cress was relocated up to the top.

About 300 feet back in the haulage or work adit is the ore dump from the work area, which is approximately 60 feet above. The ore drops downward in the chute and is controlled by a steel gate located at the bottom. The job of Dave Cress was to load ore carts from this chute and push the carts over the railroad tracks to the entry and to the top of the ore upper bunker, where the ore is then dumped

Following a few months, Cress again requested a change in jobs and this time a miner job became available as a driller in the work stope. All the drilling at the Lone Jack workings was performed by the single-jack method. In the stope (mining) area, a driller worked from his knees, as there was not space to stand. In this method, a miner works alone and held the drill with one hand and with a hammer striking the drill, rotating it at the same time.

Cress considered himself in good shape for a young man but soon discovered that this new position required unbelievable strength. It took him two to three weeks before he was performing the job for a straight 10-hour shift.

At the standard Lone Jack wage, Cress received $2 per day for a 10-hour shift at the Lone Jack and the workers received their pay once a month. Cress discovered that he hadn't been out to civilization for a long duration when he was counting nine paychecks and thus decided it was time to head out.

With the mine operating year-long, the most common problem that stopped the Lone Jack was the lack of water. By late fall, all the streams were low and the water would freeze by early winter.

There were a variety of cooks at the site that Cress recalled, one being a Swedish man. However, the one whom he thought to be the best and the one whose company he enjoyed was a Chinese cook with his half-breed Indian wife.

Safeguarding the Gold

Now that the Lone Jack was finally a producer of gold, a newly created problem surfaced about how to transport the gold from the Jack to a secure banking establishment in New Whatcom. In the years of construction and development, this item had been discussed only a few times but now created a major concern. Now with the production in full swing and the regular transportation of the gold on a monthly basis, a feasible plan was quickly required.

The man who was the superintendent of the whole operation was Sam Gilmore and the second in command was Andy Ecklund. Because of his position, Gilmore could not leave his post so Ecklund was the chosen person responsible for the gold transportation. Again the Cress brothers, John or Dave, volunteered to serve as guards to accompany Ecklund on the trips.

Mrs. Ecklund sewed a vest of lightweight canvas, with pockets made to fit the size of the flat gold bars, and Big Andy wore the vest under another type of heavy coat or rain gear. The first shipment of gold, worth $20 per ounce, had a mint value of $27,000, and weighed more than 80 pounds. In late 2005, with gold at $500 per ounce, that value was $675,000.

There was a possibility of three routes for transporting the gold out. The first route was over Twin Lakes Pass down to Shuksan and Maple Falls, followed by a train to New Whatcom. A second route went down the Chilliwack River to the city of Chilliwack, then by railroad to Sumas and then to New Whatcom. The third proposed route was south over Mamie Pass, down Ruth Creek to Shuksan, then to Maple Falls and concluded with a train trip to New Whatcom. The proposed third route over Mamie Pass was not used because the trail basically had not been improved to the level of the other two.

The amount of gold to be carried out, the man who wore the vest, the guard or guards to accompany him, the departure time and the route of travel were well-guarded secrets and generally varied with each shipment. One of the Cresses was awoken in the middle of the night with a hand covering their mouth and a tap on the shoulder to indicate he was to carry the gold or act as guard. The responsibility that fell on the Cress brothers to act as guards for the gold shipment was a heavy burden, but each fully accepted the role and handled the assignment as if they were seasoned law-enforcement agents.

On one trip out, Andy Ecklund carried the gold bars with John Cress as the assigned guard. The normal route out and the departure schedule were strict secrets with only Gilmore, Eckland and Cress aware.

The two left the mill site in the early afternoon with Ecklund in the lead and Cress a few minutes later. Both men were fully armed and Cress traveled a safe distance behind where he could constantly see Big Andy. The two men had prearranged hand signals by which either could signal the other.

With the two arriving in the town of Shuksan at Judge Broyles' Roadhouse at dusk, Big Andy settled into the roadhouse and John as always located in a separate nearby cabin. The carrier and guard at all times kept themselves separated so that no one could conceive any connection of the two.

The two continued down the North Fork Trail at about midnight with Ecklund traveling in the lead with the gold bars and a can lantern by which Cress could be signaled if necessary. Cress stumbled along behind in near-total darkness, only occasionally catching a flash of light from Ecklund's lantern. As they traveled the trail through the dense forest, one can imagine all the robbers who were possibly hiding behind every stump and tree branch.

Following the 12-mile trek down the trail, they reached the fall, and crossed the toll bridge without incident. About this hour the first streaks of daylight began to appear in the east, and as per plan, Cress increased the distance between the two. At a point, after crossing Dead Horse Creek Bridge and traveling around a sharp bend in the trail, Cress detected that Ecklund suddenly stopped with his hand covering his mouth to signal for silence. Cress waved his arm to signal an acknowledgment to Ecklund and with great caution proceeded on. Upon reaching the spot where Ecklund had stopped, John to his surprise glanced up into some small rock cliffs. There sat a man with a rifle across his lap, sound asleep. Both men quickly continued down to Glacier for the train ride to New Whatcom. Both men discussed the man in the rocks for years to come and both felt he was sitting there for one reason only: the Lone Jack gold.

Another young man about the age of the Cresses who worked at the Jack, Olaf Moline, also served as a guard and a carrier of gold bars. On one occasion in the middle of the night, Moline was notified of a gold shipment with him serving as the carrier and Ecklund to perform the guard duties. The two left in the darkness of night and spaced themselves 100 yards apart.

As they approached Shuksan, Moline, who was in the lead, lost sight of Ecklund and became concerned about what action to take. Had Ecklund been attacked and were robbers now closing in on him? The remaining two miles into Shuksan were exceedingly nerve-wracking for the young man and upon arriving he located the cabin of a trusted friend, who safely guarded the gold.

Immediately Moline headed back up the trail to see if he could locate his friend and guard. Two miles up the trail, he found Ecklund sitting quietly in the trail. In the darkness, Big Andy had walked off a corner of the trail, fell over a small cliff and broke his leg. Moline assisted Ecklund to the friend's cabin in Shuksan. Under strong orders from Ecklund, Moline continued his trip with the gold but without a guard. This was a very scary trip for a young man.

Since the Lone Jack was considered the king of the Mount Baker Mining District and the first genuine production mine, numerous prospectors were constantly stopping by for a look. All visitors were welcome to stop and take a quick look around, then were expected to move on in a short period of time.

Two prospectors who stated that they were searching for mining claims to purchase called one day and visited with some of the Jack's miners and mill workers who were off shift. About every two or three days, the two would return for another friendly visit. After seeing the repeated visits, and with an upcoming gold cleanup and gold haul out, Gilmore and Ecklund became suspicious.

On the day of the planned trip out with the gold, the friendly two arrived once more at the mine. Gilmore and

Ecklund felt that one of the workers at the operation was leaking information to these phony prospectors. Ecklund, instead of setting out at his prearranged time, secretly laid hidden with the gold shipment in the mine and remained there until the two strangers had been departed for several hours. He then headed out as customary with his guard.

Ecklund figured that the prospectors would assume that he had left without being seen, and the two set out in hot pursuit. Naturally they did not catch up with Ecklund, for he was behind them. Reaching Glacier before daylight, Ecklund and the guard went into hiding at the hotel and remained there until the train arrived. Ecklund and Cress, his guard, then sneaked out the back door of the hotel and climbed on board the departing train. As they pulled out of the station, they noticed the two "prospectors" in the crowd on the platform, too fearful of the number present to attempt a holdup.

Many years passed with Big Andy never seeing nor hearing anything of the two prospectors again. Then Ecklund received a letter from a man on his deathbed in a Chilliwack hospital who was requesting that Big Andy come visit him for he had a confession to present to him. In his confession to Ecklund on his deathbed, the man stated that he was one of the two "prospectors" at the Lone Jack and, yes, their plan that day was to rob Ecklund and Cress. The dying man smiled and added, "You out-smarted us."

News Update

The news story in the Bellingham Herald dated Jan. 25, 1904, stated the Lone Jack was operating with a 10-stamp operation with additional stamps to be added. The current 10-stamp mill then in operation generated gross revenues of $39,520 a month or practically $500,000 a year. Also, a Bellingham Herald article dated Sept. 9, 1904, stated that an additional five-stamp mill was being shipped to the Lone Jack, installed and would begin operating within three weeks (actually they were put in operation about Jan. 1, 1905).

Ecklund came to Bellingham with the cleanup for the previous month and the gold was deposited in the Bank of Bellingham for future shipment to Portland. One source reported that Ecklund arrived with about 50 pounds of gold that was worth about $15,000. The gold being shipped from the Lone Jack was similar to other mines in that it was not 100-percent pure and the quality varied from shipment to shipment. Ecklund stated that the mill was now running both night and day shifts with 35 men employed.

W.J. Keough of Baker City, Ore. was named to replace Andrew Ecklund as the mine superintendent. After all those years at the Lone Jack, Big Andy left to join with his old friend Henry Stanislawsky, who was operating the Mt. Baker and Yale Mining Co. in Canada.

Shareholder's Dividend

On Oct. 15, 1904, news came that all of the company shareholders had been patiently expecting—the day that the first dividend was to be distributed. From the time of discovery which was Aug. 21, 1897 to this date, there had not been a dividend paid. In Bellingham alone there were 90 shareholders. On this day, the Bank of Bellingham paid 2 percent of the mine's profits to the shareholders based on the number of shares owned by each individual.

Russ Lambert, one of the original owners and discoverers, was in to receive his check for $500, which he received as his share of the dividend declared. When Post, Lambert, and Van Valkenburg sold the mine to the Portland syndicate, Lambert retained 25,000 shares of the stock. Fred P. Offerman of Bellingham and S.A. Post of Concrete held considerable stock in the Mt. Baker Mining Co. Lambert stated that the Mt. Baker Mining Co. used $20,000 for purchasing the added five-stamp mills, which were almost at the site, and provisions for the coming year.

The second and third dividends of the Lone Jack were paid on Feb. 16 and June 9 of 1905 through the Bank of Bellingham. Also, the Mt. Baker Mining Co. made known that an offer to buy the operation was received but the proposal was rejected.

The Mt. Baker Mining Co. at this time owned many other mining claims in the Mount Baker Mining District other than those of the Lone Jack. On Nov. 7, 1904, Andrew Ecklund representing the Mt. Baker Mining Co. recorded the assessment work on four other claims in the area. The Cave In Rock, and the Eldorado are situated in the vicinity of the Lone Jack, and the Olga (named after his daughter) and the Red Mountain Placer were located near the border.

With all the positive information regarding the Lone Jack, the article that appeared in the Bellingham Reveille on Jan. 15, 1905 must have been a surprise and created the first negative feeling.

"Andrew Ecklund, the reinstated superintendent of the Post-Lambert mine, arrived in the city yesterday from the property. Mr. Ecklund stated to a Reveille reporter that operations were practically at a standstill at the property on account of the snow and ice and that on this account it had been found necessary to lay off half of the crew which had so far been able to work during the winter. Although Ecklund denied that he had brought down any of the cleanup of the mine for the past month, it is understood upon very good authority that he did bring down in the neighborhood of $20,000.

"Although the reporter tried to impress upon the mind of the superintendent the fact that there are stockholders in this city who are anxious to know how things are prospering at the mine, he refused to give out any information and stated that it is not the wish of the company to have any comments on the property appear in the papers. Not only does this seem to be their wish that the stockholders also know nothing of the workings of the mine. Ecklund stated that if their stockholders wished any information on the subject they could get it by writing to the head office at Portland; but either this is not the case or the stockholders do not know of it, for it is certain that there are many of them in this city who are anxious to know something of the company and its workings who so far have been unable to get a trace of this information."

News releases or any type of news from the Portland office of the Mt. Baker Mining Co., had become seriously closed-mouth concerning their operation with very sparse news stories or news of any type.

In the spring of 1905, a second tramway was completed at the Mt. Baker Mining Co. Since the discovery of the Lone Jack vein, development work periodically had been carried out on the Lulu vein, which was located to the north and at a lower elevation. The new operating plan stated that both veins would have operable trams, which were to transport ore to the common stamp mill above Silesia Creek.

Nestos & McDonald received a contract to transport the materials in a manner similar to the original tram. This second tram took the pressure off the Lone Jack vein and allowed needed further development on the Jack. By late summer of 1905, the second tramway was in operation. On Nov. 23, 1905, the Lone Jack closed again for the winter.

During 1906, the closed-mouth attitude of the Mt. Baker Mining Co. continued to provide little information concerning the Lone Jack. One story on Sept. 23, 1906 reported a missing miner. Heine Nise had journeyed to Bellingham for a needed break. Upon returning to Glacier, Nise learned that the Nooksack River was at flood stage. Reluctantly, he stayed over night in Glacier.

In the morning Nise discovered that the bridge over the river was washed out but he decided to continue toward the Jack with a plan to ford the river. That was the last anyone seen or heard from Nise and his remains were never located.

On Dec. 12, 1906, the Bellingham Reveille reported interesting news concerning the relationship between the management and shareholders: "The Whatcom County Mining Association was thrown into a furore last night by the introduction of a resolution criticizing the management at the Post-Lambert Mine, Whatcom County's first real producer of gold in the Mount Baker Mining District. J.A. Hatton, its sponsor, finally withdrew the resolution, after a lengthy and spirited discussion.

"The preamble of the resolution stated that 'lack of definite information regarding the business transactions of the Mt. Baker Mining Co. and the output and operation of the Lone Jack or Post-Lambert Mine, has caused suspicions regarding the management; that these suspicions have been and are detrimental to the mining industry

of Whatcom County and to members of the association; that because of these suspicions many people have withheld their financial and moral support from the mining industry here; that a number of members of the association are stockholders, but have no more definite information regarding the operation and business transactions of the company, value of the ore and amount of output than the public at large; that the stockholders are not allowed access to the mine and are not notified of meetings or given any statements of receipts or expenditures of the company.'

"The resolution demanded that the company furnish the association with a statement of the output, receipts and expenditures to date, and permit a representative of the association to examine the mine and mill, or take such positive action as will dispel the aforesaid suspicions. It's up to the company to be honest with the stockholders, was the comment of Hatton as his reading was completed.

"Has any stockholder ever made a complaint, inquired William Cox, acting president. It is not the privilege of the association to probe into such matters without a request from stockholders. He was informed by Secretary Bardon that there was nothing before the association except the resolution. Mr. Bardon also suggested that the stockholders get into action.

"Mr. Hatton stated that the county was suffering the effects of the black eye given it by the attitude of the company—that capital had been kept out. I'm in sympathy with the man who drafted the resolution, but we would be going further than warranted by law if in fact we demanded a statement, said Cox. We have no more right to do this than to demand a statement from any local company. At this point the resolution was tabled and no further action was taken."

The news story that was released on April 17, 1907 by the Reveille was received as a real shock to all shareholders and other parties interested in the Lone Jack: "GOLD OUTPUT IS A SURPRISE"

"In the first authentic statement ever made public, Secretary Leo Friede of the Mt. Baker Mining Co., vice president and owner of the Post-Lambert mine, states that the output in gold of the Mount Baker mine in 1906 was less than $15,000 total. The statement was made to a stockholder of the company and the letter is now in possession of an official of the Whatcom County Miner's Association. The notice of the statement, with printed remarks, will be given by the Northwestern Miner, for a time the official publication of the Washington State Mining Association.

"Secretary Friede's statement is a great surprise to local mining men, the majority of whom has always supposed the output of the Post-Lambert mill is at least $50,000 or $75,000 annually and there are many miners who think the yield of 1906 is near these figures. An official of the Whatcom County Miners Association declared there is talk of asking for a receiver for the Post-Lambert. Of this, however, two of the best-known Bellingham stockholders, R. Kline and S.A. Post, say they have not heard."

On June 28, 1907, "Instructions have been received by Andrew Ecklund, foreman of the Post-Lambert mine, to begin operations on this property again. The company has ordered him to strike the Lone Jack vein on the lower level and make a connection with the tunnel to the Lulu vein so that the one bore will be sufficient for both ledges."

Jack's Fire

The headline on Saturday, July 27, 1907 of the Reveille and the Evening America published in Bellingham read: "POST-LAMBERT STAMP MILL DESTROYED BY FIRE— WASHINGTON GREATEST CAMP IS WIPED OUT BY THE FLAMES"

"Fire, the origin of which is unknown in Bellingham, totally destroyed the Post-Lambert mine's fifteen-stamp mill, sawmill and camp buildings in the upper regions of the Mount Baker Mining District last night, entailing a loss of approximately $100,000, should it prove that the stamps were rendered useless. Even if the stamps can be utilized again the loss will be between $25,000 and $50,000, it is estimated.

"Word concerning the loss of the mill was received in Bellingham late last night from the Reveille's correspondent at Glacier. Details are lacking and it is not known whether the conflagration was started by a forest fire, as is surmised by some people, or in some other way. The only person at the mill was a watchman, all work having been abandoned a few weeks ago preparatory to the opening of the mine on a larger scale and the installation of an air compressor. Andrew Ecklund, superintendent, is now in Bellingham and probably will leave for the property today.

"Forest fires have been raging in the Mount Baker District and it is possible the watchman had a desperate battle with flames from this source. With no fire fighting apparatus and no assistance, however, he could do little. In addition to the stamps the mill building contained amalgamators, machinery, bunkhouse, cookhouse and office. Nearby was a sawmill with a daily capacity of 10,000 feet of lumber per day.

"The mill was located far up the mountain side and with the natural draught, a fire once started there would sweep with such rapidity that it would have been impossible for the watchman to summons assistance in time to prevent the destruction of the buildings, which were as dry as tinder.

"The loss of the Post-Lambert mill is a serious blow to mining in Whatcom County, particularly if the machinery is damaged beyond repair. Since the cessation of work on Slate Creek's original stamp mill, the Post-Lambert has been the most productive

mine in Northwestern Washington. When operating at full force twenty-five or thirty men were employed, to whom was disbursed $2,500 monthly in wages.

"The mine, which is about twenty miles from Glacier, was discovered in 1897 by Jack Post and R.S. Lambert and the opening of its rich ledges, the Lulu and Lone Jack, caused great excitement. In August 1903, a ten-stamp mill was placed in operation and two years later five additional stamps were installed. To purchase and install the first ten stamps the Mt. Baker Mining Co., the owners, paid $40,000. The excessive cost was due to the heavy road construction. Several thousand dollars was also invested in an aerial tramway 4,000 feet long.

"All the gold from this mine was carried from the mine to Sumas and Bellingham by Superintendent Ecklund and expressed from these cities to Portland. Not once in the four years that he bore the treasure of the hills to civilization was he molested by highwaymen.

"Many estimates relative to the output have been made, some mining men declaring that the annual production was from $100,000 to $150,000. No public statement was ever issued by the company, which has always been secretive about its affairs. The dividends have been paid, totaling $60,000, but none has been declared for more than a year. Of the 1,000,000 shares of stock about 100,000 are owned by Bellingham stockholders."

The Bellingham Herald paper dated July 27, 1907 released a similar article, but no additional information was available "It is thought that the conflagration was started by a forest fire which was raging in that district, although one report this morning stated that the camp had been fired by incendiaries." Also stated, "A tunnel was being bored from the Lulu to the Lone Jack claim, a distance of about 600 feet, and it was the intention of the company to install a large air compressor at a cost of $5,000 and the cost of building the tunnel was $6,000."

In 1932, John Cress, Olaf Moline, and Earl Hamilton, all of Whatcom County, returned to the Lone Jack Stamp Mill. Each carried a load of as many old gunnysacks as they possibly could carry. After soaking the sacks in water, they wiped up all of the sandy waste material on the floor area of the burned-out mill. Then a hot fire was built in a barrel to burn the sacks. After all of the sacks had been burned, the three went through the remains, recovering all the sandy materials. The next step in the operation required hand-panning the material in gold pans and each came home with $200.

Chapter 6
Brooks-Willis

Boundary Gold Company

Following the devastating fire in the summer of 1907, the Lone Jack mill and mine fell into a state of disrepair with the effects of winter's long months taking their toll. The fire, in sweeping through the mill site, had not totally destroyed all of the buildings but considerable damage had incurred to the mine building.

The Mt. Baker Mining Co. had switched from the Lone Jack workings to the Lulu workings and had placed in service a second tramway to the Lulu. In the following years, one or two men were stationed at the site in the summer months to safeguard the interest of the Mt. Baker Mining Co. If these men were not guarding the site, thieves would have freely dug through the open workings and the waste pile down at the mill site. There is no record that the Mt. Baker Mining Co. performed any further work beyond this time at the Lone Jack.

On Feb. 25, 1913, the Mt. Baker Mining Co. reached an agreement to sell the Lone Jack to George Thomas and S.Q. Clark for a price of $75,000. This sale included all the patented claims, non-patented claims, all equipment as is, and all buildings as they stood.

Thomas and Clark formed the Boundary Gold Co. and placed this operation into their new corporation. The Boundary Gold Co. was incorporated in Portland, Ore. The agreement listed the following items: "all machinery and tools, stamp mill, sawmill, tramway, timber, bunkhouse, cabins, and all ore, mill tailing and concentrates thereon, also the Whist Creek and Garrison Creek Water Power improvements, together with pipe line, penstock, water wheel etc."

These new owners were as inadequately informed about the condition of the weather and winter snowfall in the Cascade Mountains as the first owners, the Mt. Baker Mining Co. On the first page, the agreement states that the purchasers will "Enter upon said mining property on or before the first day of May 1913, to begin, practical and economic mining work on the same; that not less than seventy-five shifts of labor shall be performed on said properties during each month after said first of May, 1913, and in the event that said work be rendered impractical through climatic or other conditions beyond the control of the Purchasers, that they will, in the months following thereafter, do sufficient work to maintain said average during the year." Also it was stated, "Commence as soon as weather conditions permit, have complied and in actual operation on or before Nov. 1, 1913, on said property a mill with the capacity of not less than twenty tons per day, and that they will increase the capacity of said mill as rapidly as the development of said properties will justify."

The terms of payment of the $75,000 was to be $25,000 due four years from the date of the agreement, the second payment of $25,000 payable one year from the date of the first, and the third and last payment of $25,000 to be made one year after the second payment. The agreement had clauses, which said that the purchasers were to pay a royalty to the Mt. Baker Mining Co. of 12.5 percent of the gross mill smelter or mint receipts to the time of the first payment. This royalty was not to apply as part of the first payment and did not apply after the first payment.

The development of the Boundary Gold Co. commenced on the Lulu lead. This was a location that the Mt. Baker Mining Co. had mined previously, yet still required a large amount of development work. At the time of the devastating fire, the shipment of the ore to the stamp mill by the tramway was traveling from the Lulu.

Thomas and Clark erected processing equipment at the portal of the Lulu adit and constructed two cliff-hanging buildings; one for the mill equipment and a second as a bunkhouse/cookhouse. (This location is at the first adit at the Lulu, which is currently caved, and where the aluminum irrigation pipe currently lies). These two structures hung off the rock with drilled anchors and steel cables. The position of the buildings was such that avalanches passed to one side or the other.

Boundary Gold Co. ore mill & cook/bunk house 1915. (J. Munroe)

Boundary Gold Co. completed structure. (S. Post-Plummer)

By 1913, conditions on Bear Mountain were not improved from the 1900 operation. After the fire at the Lone Jack Mill, all equipment that was intended to be reused existed 1,500 feet down the hill with all of the trails having slid shut and brush had grown covering them. Only a small amount of milling equipment was moved up and relocated at the new operation, which required a totally new process; however, any items needed for the cook-bunkhouse were transported to the new site. The road up the North Fork of the Nooksack River had been improved, but the trail up Swamp Creek lacked improvements.

Murder at the Lone Jack

In the winter of 1916/1917, the Boundary Gold Co. ceased operation for the winter. The company had hired two local men to be employed to prevent any thievery from occurring, as it had in the past. Martin Orner a likeable sort of a Swede who had been employed at the Lone Jack in years past, and Tony Copan, an Italian were hired for the winter job. Orner and Copan, both Glacier residents, received no salary, but in lieu of salary the two were free to mine and mill as much gold by hand as possible during the winter and have free access to company stores in the cookhouse. With winter approaching, the two said farewells to all their friends in Glacier, and headed out to establish housekeeping for the six months of winter at the Jack.

With these introductory remarks, we are shut off from the two foreign men with contrasting blood, features and language who must pass the long winter by themselves, with only the gold in the mine to act as keeper of the peace. On a rainy day in the following spring, a tired, bedraggled Copan arrived at the McDonalds's Store in Glacier. After the men in the store received and greeted Copan, the next obvious question from all was: "Where is Orner?"

Copan answered slowly with a strong Italian accent. He said Orner went off hunting for deer three weeks past and had yet to make a return. Copan's story related that he had gone out searching for Orner the next few days but was unsuccessful in finding any trace of him. Then, after finally giving up hope with a lapse of considerable time and the need to notify the authorities, Copan returned to Glacier with the story, his personal gear and the total gold of both men.

Frank Bottiger, a special friend of Orner, and other Glacierites felt that Copan was hiding the truth. So a group of Orner's friends decided to perform their own investigation at the Jack and force Copan to return with them. Copan indicated that he clearly wasn't going back but Bottiger forcefully persuaded him to return with the group. Upon searching one or two days at the site, seeing nothing that indicated any type of foul play, the group returned to Glacier and released Copan to freedom. Within two days, Copan slipped out of Glacier with the two shares of gold—never to be seen again.

A few years later, Bert Lowry, an old-time prospector and trapper, was prospecting in the Twin Lakes area and traveled to the now-quiet Jack for a look around. Entering the Lulu shaft with a light, he noticed a floating object in a mined-out winze, which was full of seepage water.

After a closer look, Lowry determined that the floating object was in fact a man's body. He quickly recalled the disappearance of Martin Orner. The body had been tied with rope to large rocks and thrown in the water hole. Over a period of time, the rope had rotted through and the body floated to the surface.

Lowry returned to Glacier. A group of Orner's friends, headed by Bottiger, returned with Lowry to the mine. They recovered the body and the group gave Orner the best burial possible in an almost solid rock soil on the side of Bear Mountain hillside. The Whatcom County sheriff was notified by Bottiger upon their return to Glacier and a statewide search for Copan was called. The sheriff followed his trail to Seattle, where he deposited the gold into the United States Assay Office for $1,500, but no further trace of Copan's location was ever found beyond Seattle.

Failure of Boundary Gold Co.

Leo Friede, secretary of the Mt. Baker Mining Co., wrote a letter extending the terms of payment by Boundary Gold Co. from those noted above. The letter called for the first payment on Feb. 25, 1920, the second on Feb. 25, 1921, and the third on Feb. 25, 1922 with the stipulation that one Lane Slow Speed Chilean Mill be added to the site with daily capacity of 25-30 tons per day.

Friede also wrote in this letter: "Mining at all times is a problem judging by our experience, and that you may find favorable indications at one place, and not so much at another is but the experience of all people that develop mines. But when we go back in thought and recall the rich ore we found on the Lone Jack vein, we cannot believe that it lay in the one spot, and nearly all mining men confirm our hopes by saying the matter of a fault in mines is unknown, and it is only a question of development when we may again pick up the lead."

On Feb. 24, 1916, the agreement was amended again, moving the payment dates to Feb. 25, 1923, Feb. 25, 1924, and Feb. 25, 1925. The agreement had requirements that were listed as follows: "change the power plant now on the property by placing a new power wheel thereon and extending the steel flume a distance of approximately nine hundred and fifty feet toward Silesia Creek for power purposes and if necessary to build a flume about one mile long from Silesia Creek to the power plant referred to. You will also replace the copper wire now in use for transmission purposes to steel wire from the power plant to the mine and you will also install two additional power drills."

Warner Dahlmen, Gus Dahlmen, and Niles Helms were hired on

Oct. 1, 1913, at the Lone Jack by George Thomas and S.Q. Clark, who represented the Boundary Gold Co. Their pay was to be $3 per eight-hour day plus board. These men were in their late 20's or early 30's, from Anaconda, Mont., and were experienced miners. The three men were hired through B.B. Employment Agency in Bellingham and were required each to pay the agency $1.50 for the service. The three miners were employed for a total of 286 days and on July 14, 1914, quit working due to the lack of payment. This information indicates that the three worked steady every day from start to finish.

During this period of employment, their work consisted of building an addition to the mill building and bunkhouse. Outside the mine, they cut timber into logs and finished construction of the buildings. The trio also worked inside the mine, blasting and breaking ore.

It soon became apparent that the three were having a problem receiving their wages. However, keep in mind that the three were working in the middle of winter in a remote area miles from the home office of Boundary Gold in Seattle. On March 24, 1914, Gus Dahlmen traveled by foot out to Glacier and on to Seattle. In the Seattle office he located Clark, who was shocked to see him. After a long discussion, Dahlmen was told that a new supply of cash was expected from a source in Colorado. Dahlmen reluctantly returned to work at the Lone Jack.

His record of payment was: March 24, $20; March 25, $20; March 26, $30; April 7, $5; April 10, $30; May 5, $21. Dahlmen also was paid merchandise worth $30 and with gold bullion worth $221.76. Also, Helms received $110 and Warner Dahlmen received $110. With this information, there is a clear record that the mill was producing gold bullion, which was sold to Faulkenberg and Laucks of Seattle. The matter of the labor lien filed by these three men was held in Superior Court of Whatcom County and found in favor of the plaintiffs. The Boundary Gold Co. was ordered to pay all remaining past wages and all expenses. The Mt. Baker Milling Co. was dismissed as defendant in the case.

The Boundary Gold Co. had the identical problem that plagued the Mt. Baker Mining Co. in the beginning: lack of capital. L.D. Sperry, being an owner of some degree, was elected president of the Boundary Gold Co. As in their efforts to pay the Dahlman brothers and Helms, Boundary Gold repeatedly stated that added resources were expected from Colorado.

Brooks Family

The money was not to be received from Colorado but arrived instead from a party in Portland by the name of Phillip Brooks. In 1919 Josephine Brooks provided the funds to her son Phillip, who became involved with the Jack and over the next few years Phillip Brooks became the sole owner.

Josephine Brooks trip to the Orient. (E. Dick)

Josephine Brooks, with her husband Lester Brooks, resided in Portland, Ore. The wealthy Brooks family had interests in many business ventures all over the Pacific Northwest and Josephine was the driving force. She had a family connection with the Bullene family in Whatcom County.

In the beginning, Phillip Brooks may have been a partner at some level with the Boundary Gold Co. He paid off the $75,000 that was the price in the agreement with Mt. Baker Mining Co. It is assumed that Phillip made the payments as shown in the last extension that was granted to Boundary Gold by Mt. Baker Mining and the last payment of $25,000 was completed Feb. 25, 1925.

Brooks-Willis Metals, Inc. was incorporated in the State of Washington on Aug. 24, 1924 with Phillip Brooks and Carl Willis named as trustees and a listed capital of $160,000. Willis, a mining engineer, was placed totally in charge of the development work and

Phillip Brooks. (E. Dick)

The Brooks residence in Portland, Ore. (E. Dick)

mining operation. The first act that Willis performed was filing nine additional non-patented claims that he named Willis No. 1, Brooks No. 1, Diplomacy, Q.C.R., Carl, Phillip, Samuel, Ranney, and Donna.

With these added claims and the originals, Brooks and Willis now controlled over 270 acres. Brooks, the businessman, positioned himself in charge of the financial needs with family funds and other available sources.

Willis announced that he was acting as a representative of Phillip Brooks and has purchased the Lone Jack Mine from Mt. Baker Mining Co., comprised of Hahn, Friede and other stockholders. Willis added that he had spent one year in exploration and test work at the Jack. Starting around July 15, a labor force of approximately 50 men will be employed working three shifts a day.

All the applications and hiring of new employees will be handled through Kirk Fletcher of the Brunswick Employment Agency, Dock Street, Bellingham.

The Lone Jack group consists of five original claims and extensions staked by Willis during his exploration work, giving the group 11 claims. He also has purchased two claims adjacent to the Red Mountain Gold Mill. Development work will be concentrated on the Lone Jack claims this year.

Willis states, "It's the intent of the Lone Jack Co. to ship all ores through Bellingham, although this can only be accomplished by cooperation on the part of the county commissioners in assisting road facilities. If nothing is done, the ores will necessarily have to be shipped through Sardis, B.C. We want to do all business through this city and at present we are having

LONE JACK MINE, ASSAY SHEET.

Nov. 18, 1921

LULU LODE

No.	Weight Gold	Weight Silver	Total Value	Location of Sample.
JA	0.58	0.22	$11.82	Large stope near end of cross-out from poi half way up raise. Northwest end of stope. Width sampled, 33 in., quartz
TTT	3.28	0.70	66.30	Small stope at end of cross out from raise. At point in bottom of stope level with rai and facing it. Sample taken from 3 bands of scattered sulphides, each 4 in. thick. Widt of vein at this point, 40 in.
LD	0.51	0.17	10.57	From same locality as TTT. Represents 3 in. next to hanging wall.
JM	0.23	0.09	4.69	Same stope as JA. East end of stope. Width of vein 46 in.
HC	0.64	0.30	13.10	Same locality as JM. Represents 20 in. of schist with gash veins of quartz, occurring in lower portion of vein next to footwall, under sample JM
JG	.40	0.12	9.12	Large upper stope with openings to surface. Lowest part of stope at northwest end width sampled, 6 ft. of quartz. 30 ft west o cross-out leading from top of raise into stope
KKK	1.39	.53	28.13	From outcrop of vein(LULU) 100 ft. west of last opening into stope. width sampled, 2 f Average width of vein at this locality 1½ f

OUTCROP NEAR LONE JACK TRAIL

HJ	0.59	0.25	$12.05	Short tunnel opened on quartz vein in fine gray dike rock. Above trail between Lulu and Lone Jack workings

LONE JACK LODE

HA	1.51	0.31	31.33	From large stope reached by chute which opens beside raise from adit level. Bottom of stope, southeast side of chute, at corne
GH	0.94	0.46	19.06	Small stope with chute opening about 110 ft. southeast of raise from adit level. NW sid of stope. Width sampled, 2 ft., quartz and gangue.

Lone Jack Mine assay sheet Nov. 18, 1921. (C. Stone)

considerable machinery built here with which to operate the development work this summer.

"The road to the Lone Jack passes through Glacier, Shuksan and extends seven miles over the Twin Lakes Trail and the site is located on the shoulder of Bear Mountain." Willis continued.

"At about twice the cost of an ordinary forestry pony trail, a road sufficient to haul ores out with a narrow caterpillar tractor can be effective, it is said. At present, supplies which are being bought in Bellingham are shipped by bond through Canadian Territory and taken in over the Sardis Trail."

100

When asked about the future operation, Willis added, "The Lone Jack has had a black eye in the past and I am sure this is because of gross ignorance on the part of those who have operated the mine. They mined more for free gold than anything else, and there is a gold telluride in the ore that is worth many times more than the free gold alone. The free gold equals about 10 percent of the value of the ore per ton. This has been proven by a series of laboratory tests made in Vancouver, B.C. and the concentrates are worth $2,500 per ton.

"The intent is to install an oil flotation system at the site of the mine this year and use the machinery now in place until bigger developments are made," Willis said. "It also is our intent to operate the small sawmill near the property with which to build homes for miners and their families. The water plant now on Silesia Creek will be brought farther down and a larger water wheel installed. Other machinery will be put in as soon as the development of the mine warrants it.

"The Lone Jack will be operated 12 months of the year and is said to be one of the driest mines to work in the part of the country, which is considered a coincidence as the Red Mountain Gold Mine is known to be "wet." Equipment will soon be installed that will give the Lone Jack the capacity of 300 tons per day, although 50 or 60 tons per day would be mined."

Willis has been a mining engineer for the past 28 years and was prominent in the development of the Porcupine and Cobalt Mining Districts of Ontario. He has also been connected officially with a large New York mining company and was doing exploration work for an Eastern concern a year ago, when he first saw the Lone Jack. Realizing, as he said, that the telluride values were extremely high, he made further examination, which convinced him that the Glacier District (Mt. Baker District) was valuable in gold ore and highly mineralized throughout the whole district.

Willis concluded, "There is a great future for the Glacier or Mt. Baker Mining Districts if the people will get behind them and we are not selling any stock, but have waged our all to prove that the Lone Jack Mine is what we believe it to be. We are told that the Lone Jack has produced $192,000 in gold and it hasn't been scratched, that does not represent one-tenth of what there is in sight."

The past milling operation of the Lone Jack lead was done to the south of Lulu Gulch. Willis decided that the operation of the Lulu Lead would basically be located on the north side of Lulu Gulch, a major avalanche chute starting on the top of Bear Mountain and flowing down to Silesia Creek, a distance of 1.5 miles. Each winter this area is swept clean and the snow buildup at the creek bottom can reach 40 feet deep. The decision of Willis was apparently made because of the constant danger of men crossing this area in the winter and spring.

In the summer of 1922, with the start of the Brooks operation quickly reaching high gear with a large work force, the activity at the old Jack would have been unbelievable. Charlie Bourn, the main Glacier packer with about 35 animals, moved freight at an amazing rate. In the early periods, there were as many as two packtrains arriving and departing each day from the Lone Jack. The freight was received at the Lone Jack Freight Depot at Shuksan by trucks.

With Willis having been around the Jack for a few years and being aware of the short season, all major forms of activity were started as soon as the snow melted. It would be assumed there was a construction labor force of about 50 men and another 10 men as support personnel.

The chief item with starting of the development and construction was the establishment of a base camp to house and feed the workers. With the existing Lone Jack Mill Site bunkhouse and cookhouse having not burned when the fire destroyed the mill and other structures, this was to provide the base camp for the Brooks-Willis operation. In the beginning, the clearing and rebuilding of the existing trails was needed as the years had taken their toll.

One of the first items of business was a new modern No. 1 American sawmill with a daily capacity of 5,000 board feet. It was erected on the Silesia Creek Trail in the middle of an old-growth area of Alaska Cedar. The mill was powered by a small Cleveland bulldozer. This bulldozer was placed in a permanent position as the need for the sawmill was for the duration of the operation. All the cut lumber was moved from the mill to the needed construction site by horse dragging as none of the trails was constructed wide enough or straight enough for a wagon of any type.

The electric generating powerhouse was located down the hill below the sawmill site and placed in the hillside 100 feet above Silesia Creek. The water source that powered the Impulse Pelton Wheel was diverted from Garrison and Whist creeks, which cascaded down Lulu Gulch. The two creeks had intensive hand ditching to channel both streambeds together to form one channel to capture all available water. This water, regulated by a solid wood control gate, was channeled into an almost flat grade wood flume, which flowed across the hillside for about a third of a mile.

At the end of the flume, the water flowed down a penstock with a vertical drop of 500 feet, which was constructed of steel hoop wood pipe. The water then rotates the pelton wheel, which operates a 2,800 volt, DC 50 kilowatt (60 cycle) generator. This power source provided power for all machinery at the Brooks-Willis operation.

The other electric installations included telephone and electric wiring with lighting in the mill, power plant, assay and general office. The telephone connects the mine, mill, powerhouse, sawmill and office. All of

```
Bellingham  Shuksan Freight.

F.S.Chandler, Maple Falls, Wn.

In B'ham Tel. 84,
   c/o Union Auto Fght Depot.
       1310 R.R.Ave.

All Freight including powder with
   no minimums charged -

B'ham - Shuksan          $10. per Ton.

Concentrates-
   Shuksan - B'ham        9.   "    "


Fght - Glacier - Shuksan 3.50"   "
Cnoc - Shuksan - Glacier 3.50"   "




Chas, Bourne,  Glacier, Wash.

Fght - Shuksan to Lone Jack Mine
       by Pony pack-------- 2¢ per lb

Concentrates on return trip will
   come some cheaper.
```

Auto freight & horsepack quotation, 1922.
(WWU-CPNWS)

Auto court at Shuksan, 1923 or 1924.
(J. Munroe)

Looking down Lulu Gulch across Silesia
Creek to Skagit Range. (C. Rousseau)

Bear Mountain, Sept. 8, 1922 Brooks-Willis
hired a professional unknown photographer
to record the development of the operation.
History started with this picture No. 1.
(J. Munroe)

Lower trail to the Brooks-Willis Ore Mill crossing Lulu Gulch with a bridge over Whist Creek. (J. Munroe)

Looking across Lulu Gulch to the Stamp Mill site that became a temporary camp for Brooks-Willis. (J. Munroe)
Point A) is the location of the stamp mill that burnt in 1907. Point B) shows temporary buildings. Point C) shows the area which was cleared in 1902.

Harry Bullene returned from the war to work at the Lone Jack. (J. Munroe)

Cook & meat house is a frame building with canvas sheeting and a pipe delivers cold mountain water to the roof which runs over the canvas thus cooling the interior. Cook is cutting up a hind quarter of beef on a tree stump. (J. Munroe)

Pack train arriving at the temporary camp. (J. Munroe)

Sawmill which was powered by a small dozer motor. (J. Munroe)

Teamsters & horses moving lumber up the trail. (J. Munroe)

Flume for powerhouse. (J. Munroe)
Point A) forest fire prior to start of Brooks-Willis. Point B) trail coming down to temporary camp. Point C) taking water from Lulu Gulch to the Penstock.

Crew assembling the electric water power plant. (J. Munroe)

Water power plant with all major equipment in place. (J. Munroe)
Point A) outlet of the Penstock.
Point B) pelton wheel. Point C) DC generator.

Men constructing wood flume. (J. Munroe)

Power plant with a complete building around it. This building provided protection for the equipment and housing for the one or two employees. (J. Munroe)

Inside the pelton wheel. (T. Anderson)
Point A) brass nozzle where water enters. This high pressure water hits pelton cup. Point B) that causes rotation which provides the power to the generator.

Governor unit that controls the amount of water entering the unit. (T. Anderson)

this is connected to the mine office and freight depot in Shuksan. A complete power plant building (26 feet x 30 feet) was built over the machinery and provides complete living quarters for one or two workers. The operation of the power plant was critical to the total operation and the necessity of keeping the flume clear of debris and water flowing was of utmost importance.

Willis realized the impracticality of hauling out concentrated ore by packhorse and decided that an ore processing plant was needed if the operation was to be successful. After choosing the mill site, Willis relocated the existing labor force to the site and started using this site as a base of operation. Willis for some reason placed the mill site out in the middle of the avalanche chute. However, he placed it directly below three or four old-growth firs—thus assuming that it was a safe spot.

Next, two small A-frame buildings were constructed, the assay office and the office building. The assay office, from the beginning of the Lulu mining operation, was necessary to make an analysis of the ore being mined. The livery barn, was then constructed to house a few of the many horses and provide coverage for the hay and other feed. In the Silesia Creek Valley, there is absolutely no natural feed for the workhorses.

A cookhouse and bunkhouse were built on the side hill north of the assay office at the same level. These two buildings could not have endured the following winter because their placement was directly in the center of the Lulu Gulch avalanche chute. Pictures show the buildings in place one year; however, the following year they were gone. The two were probably used as temporary buildings and were torn down with the lumber being reused the following season.

By Sept. 20, 1922, there stood nothing but the framework of what was to be the cookhouse at the location of the future mill. Later, after the snow drove them out for the winter, probably about Thanksgiving, the enclosed mill building was complete. The building measured about 24 feet wide, 114 feet long, and about 45 feet high at the highest point.

In the middle of the following winter (1923), Willis became worried about how well the structures were holding up with the heavy snow loads. He dispatched a party of six or seven men to investigate. One member of the party was a photographer, and his pictures indicated major damage to the mill building. The back or uphill end was completely destroyed and the downhill portion, which is the high area, was knocked out of plumb. There was nothing this party could do about the damage and they returned to Bellingham with the bad news.

In 1923, the mill building that was not destroyed that winter was completely rebuilt in a different shape. The downhill section was rebuilt and a new upper section was constructed in shed design. This new area housed the ore bin and also housed the cooking and bunkhouse for 30 men.

Unloading supplies at upper cook house at Brooks-Willis mine site. (J. Munroe)

Top end of mine building served as cook/bunk house. (J. Munroe)

Lulu Gulch with buildings. (J. Munroe)
Point A) next location of cookhouse & bunkhouse. Point B) stable.

Bunkhouse & cookhouse. The following year these buildings were no longer standing. Did a winter avalanche destroy them or were they taken down for needed lumber. (J. Munroe)

Cooks with meat cooler on the right. (J. Munroe)

Looking at north end of bunkhouse. (J. Munroe)

It contained the cook's range and culinary articles, dormitory wire-frame beds, camp heater and other items.

At this point, all of the machinery was installed in the mill. The equipment was a "Willis Mill" (30 tons capacity per 24 hours), amalgamating plates, a Dodge crusher, and two specially constructed Oil Flotation Tanks. We assume that the "Willis Mill," which was a rod mill, was the design of Carl Willis. The upper ore bin and the 696-foot aerial tramline with buckets connecting the upper and lower bins was ready to be placed in service. An Ingersol Rand compressor with airlines and accessories provided air to the mill and the mine adit area. By the completion of the mill facilities, the mining crew had been mining for some time with 650 feet of track laid and a reserve of mined ore stored on site.

In late fall of 1923, the Lone Jack once again commenced producing gold. The amount that was produced is not known. Not being satisfied with results, Phillip Brooks hired Francis Crossland, a Vancouver, B.C., mining engineer, to analyze the complete operation. The major finding of Crossland was that the slow Willis rod mill was only 50 percent efficient as to size. He recommended that the old Lane Mill up the hillside at the site of the Boundary Gold operation should be added as an auxiliary crusher with two added giant crushers.

Brooks immediately ordered the mill shut down and this work performed. The first item was to completely remove the high roof section of the mill building and construct a shed roof all sloping down hill. A completely revised layout of the existing equipment was updated and then the added pieces of equipment were installed. With the arrival of winter about Thanksgiving, the building construction and the equipment work were complete.

The Crossland report gave many interesting facts about the Lulu vein of the Lone Jack Mine:

1. As of this date Nov. 10, 1923, there has been 2,300 feet of development done in the Lulu comprising of adits, drifts, crosscuts, and stopes.

2. There was a total of 63 samples taken for assay review and the highest tested was $253.60 per ton at $20 per ton ore.

3. The assay reports indicate that the gold content was high in places and lean in others.

4. The un-stoped ore in place ranges from $20 to $25 per ton.

5. The amount of ore mined (stockpiled) and not milled is valued at $142,138.

6. Cost numbers from the Boundary Red Mountain Mine indicate their cost of the mining to $3.78, milling at $1.17 and general expense of $1.15 for a total $6.10 per ton and the Jack should be able to operate with these expenses.

January inspection party, 1923. (J. Bullene)

By the end of 1922 the mill was a closed-in building. However, as they approached severe damage was obvious. (J. Munroe)

The left side had been hit by an avalanche. (J. Munroe)

Assay office collapsed the same winter.
(J. Munroe)

Upper ore bunker which was the top end of the
tramway in the fall of 1923. (J. Bullene)

Winter 1923 wall of snow in May down at
Silesia Creek. (J. Munroe)

Crew is digging out the Lulu portal in May.
(J. Bullene)

Rebuilt mill building. (J. Munroe)
Point A) winter damage area. Point B) tramway lower discharge. Point C) temporary cook/bunk house.

Assay office and general office buried in snow middle of May 1925. (J. Munroe)

7. All the pillars are pay ore, and consideration should be given to their milling value, as it would pay to withdraw the same and install other roof supports.

8. Tunnel through Bear Mountain and come out on the west side above the headwaters of Swamp Creek. By using this tunnel for all traffic, the high pass at Twin Lakes would be eliminated.

9. The value of all the work performed to date for buildings, equipment, and other expenses is conservatively estimated at $100,000 and with the value of obtainable ore at the site the operation should be able to run for years at a profit.

On May 18, 1924, the Lone Jack finally made its first cleanup of bullion in 17 years, and reported that the mill and mine are both continually operating three shifts daily. The Maple Falls Leader reported, "On June 13, 1924, the second cleanup was verified and it is said that it is twice as large as the first. The recorded value taken out under the Brooks-Willis amounted to $18,770. The company operates a pack train to the mine daily and Willis announces that Dr. Henderson of Bellingham is engaged as company physician and will be in charge of the company hospital. The forty men employed at the mine will continue to enjoy the protection and benefits of the State Industrial Insurance."

The Jack operated intermittently in 1924 with the problem being the lack of water. This operation required a large volume of water and by early fall the water in Whist Creek completely dried. Fortunately the Mt. Baker Mining Co. had done a superior job of previously selecting its mill location and was able to use water from Silesia Creek.

Constructed in 1924, the three-tier bunkhouse was located uphill and to the south of the mill building. On the back of a photo dated May 15, 1925, showing the bunkhouse, it states "BUNK HOUSE-LONE JACK MINE." This house is built in bents and set into the hill making it safe in every respect. A slide could do no worse than pass over it but it is not in the course of slides. This is the finest mine bunk house in the State of Washington with full accommodations for sleeping and feeding 100 men. Baths and laundry, etc. included."

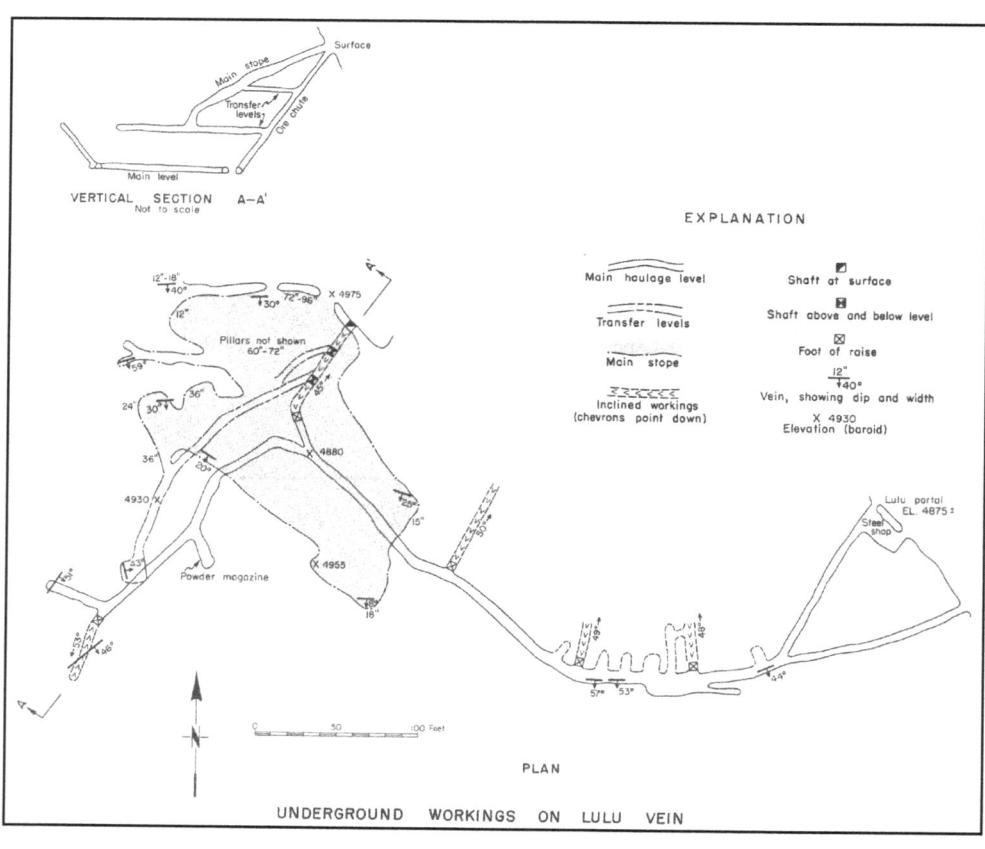

Map of complete underground workings on Lulu vein. (C. Stone)

Building with collapsed uphill section mid May 1923. (J. Munroe)

Page 121 to 124 A series of pictures that show all the different configurations of the building at the Brooks-Willis ore mill. This picture is taken in the late fall of 1922. (J. Munroe)

Same building looking from the south January 1923. (J. Munroe)

Building with newly constructed ore hopper June 1923. Note man installing roofing paper. (J. Munroe)

The roof system now has a shed roof on the upper part and peak on the downhill end. Late October 1923. (J. Munroe)

To the left of the building is the terraced foundation for the future bunkhouse. October 1923. (J. Munroe)

Summer 1924. Total shed roof. (J. Munroe)

Building from the south. Full shed roof ore hopper with lower tramway station January 1925. (J. Bullene)

Mill building and cook/bunk house May 15, 1925. (J. Munroe)

South side of cook/bunk house May, 1925. (J. Bullene)

Both buildings standing August 1932. (F. Ruzicka)

Most of the mill building has collapsed, however the cook/bunk house is standing October 1935. (B. Peters)

Mill building is gone with the lower tier of the cook/bunk house. New section built above. (B. Peters)

In the winter of 1925 a large avalanche roared off Bear Mountain, missing the mill and bunkhouse but depositing a wall of snow and ice in Silesia Creek 40 feet high. This slide destroyed the head gate and the entire portion of the flume, which was constructed in the avalanche chute. All records indicate that this was the end of Brooks-Willis Metals operation. The lack of year-round operating water, poor placement of the mill and bunkhouse, and the lack of funds through the family or from other sources were the downfall for Brooks-Willis. Also, another factor in the failure was the lack of manpower caused by World War I and a decline in gold prices. Reported production during the last year of operation (1924) was 907 ounces of gold and 38 ounces of silver from 1,557 tons of mined ore from the Lulu vein.

By Oct. 24, 1935, the majority of the mill building had collapsed and two-thirds of the bunkhouse remained standing. Under the employment of Mrs. Brooks, Harry Bullene, a nephew of Mrs. Brooks who was first employed at the Lone Jack in 1922, hired a group of Meridian High School students. Their work involved performing maintenance, such as trying to save the bunkhouse, trail work, and assessment on the non-patented claims. This took place from 1935 to 1940.

Vern Schow and Bud Peters were two of the students who worked at the Jack over two or three summer vacations. These young men were paid a wage of 30 cents to 50 cents per hour and worked continuously for three months. The crew lived in the old bunkhouse and for entertainment in the evenings they would shoot the pack rats that lived with them in the bunkhouse. Mrs. Brooks hired a man with a small narrow-gauge bulldozer in 1939 to widen the trail to the lakes, making it suitable for Jeep traffic.

In the summer of 1939 or 1940, a group of four geology/mining students from Boulder, Colo., arrived in the area and with the use of a small bulldozer reopened the trail down to the Lone Jack Stamp Mill. Following the use of the bulldozer to move the machinery and debris from the old mill site footprint, the group installed a sluice box and set to work on the old waste pile below the mill. It was reported that one summer the four recovered enough gold to put all four

though the rest of their college years. Who gave the four the approval to do this recovery? No one was to know, and Mrs. Brooks, the owner, may not have had the current right because the old mill site was not on any of her patented claims.

The Brooks operation was similar to its predecessor in the fact that they also had many legal problems. The Giant Powder Co. was awarded a suit in Superior Court of Whatcom County on Jan. 10, 1924, and Brooks-Willis was ordered to pay a dynamite invoice. The invoice was for 710 cases of dynamite with tape fuses and caps.

On June 27, 1923, Clyde Equipment filed a complaint against Phillip Brooks and Carl Willis, doing business as the Lone Jack Mine, for the sale of equipment. The amount due was $277.86 and five other creditors assigned their claims to Clyde Equipment, making the total of the claim $880.16. These creditors and the amount of their claims are listed as follows: (1) Kramer doing business

The cook/bunk house receiving maintenance work from Harry Bullene's crew in 1937 or 1938. Note cables wrapped around the structure holding it from sliding downhill. (B. Peters)

Two men working on forge. Man on the right is Bud Peters. (B. Peters)

121

Bullene crew. Bud Peters in the center.
(B.Peters)

The plaintiff alleged that there was a large number of creditors, and the total of the indebtedness was more that $40,000 and that said co-partnership was thoroughly insolvent and wholly unable to pay its debts. The complaint stated that Carl Willis had no financial responsibility in the partnership and that Phillip Brooks is reputed to be worth $1 million. Brooks was residing in Vancouver, B.C., and it was impossible to get a process served upon him. The complaint asks that the court appoint a receiver to take charge of and manage the assets. The court ruled in favor of the plaintiff and the amount was paid.

in Bellingham sold and delivered goods, wares and merchandise value at $45.10 in the summer of 1922; (2) L.E. Haggard doing business in Maple Falls sold and delivered goods, wares and merchandise for a value of $68.75; (3) E. Bowtwell performed freighting service for a value of $185.45; (4) S.D. White of Bellingham sold and delivered merchandise at a value of $76; (5) C.H. Bourn of Glacier packed freight to and from the said Lone Jack Mine to Glacier for a value of $227.

With another failure, that of the Brooks-Willis Metal Inc., the whole Lone Jack once again dropped into a period of inactivity with all operation ceased. For a period of time, assessment work was performed on the 11 unpatented claims, but slowly one after another the ownership reverted back to the government.

Phillip Brooks died on July 23, 1940, and the total holdings of the Lone Jack were inherited by his mother Josephine.

Work portal of the Lulu on the right with the blacksmith tunnel on the left—the existing aluminum pipe is the location of the Boundary Gold Co. Mill. (G. Byeman)

Air vent holes at the Lulu. (G. Byeman)

Main portal at the Lulu. (M. Impero)

Lulu adit with air line laying on the floor. (J. Christenson)

Lulu adit with trackage. (J. Christenson)

System of wood ladder to be used as manway. (J. Christenson)

Ore cart sitting still over eighty years. (G. Byeman)

124

Piled waste rock or good stuff near ore cart track. (G. Byeman)

Large pillar with quartz vein. (G. Byeman)

Lulu stoped out area. (G. Byeman)

Lane or Chilean grinding mill at the Lulu. (G. Byeman)

Jaw crusher rusting away. (G. Byeman)

Finish grinding rod mill at Lulu. (G. Byeman)

Chapter 7

Later Years

With the death of Josephine Brooks in the mid 1940's, in Portland, Harry and Mamie Bullene of Bellingham inherited the total ownership of all the property and other assets of the Lone Jack operation. This gift must have created mixed feelings for the Bullenes. Harry Bullene, who had toiled at the mine off and on for many years, had seen the heartache, disappointment, and devastation caused by the severe North Cascade winters.

Upon receiving the property, the Bullenes believed that Carl Willis, the partner in Brooks-Willis Metals, had some degree of ownership. After investigating, they discovered that Willis was a partner in title only. The Bullenes felt that this was unjust and quickly created a quit claim deed granting one-eighth ownership to Willis. Years later, the Willis family returned the property to the Bullene family.

Bullene Family Ownership

Robert Cole's main focus in the early years of his lease on the Lone Jack was to construct a mess hall-bunkhouse building with a shop attached. His crew tore down the old 1924 bunkhouse, which by this time was in a state of major disarray. The new building was built in the area of

Looking east to the five switchbacks which climb a thousand feet to Twin Lakes in less than a mile. (Ford Times)

Maneuvering one of the switchback turns. (Ford Times)

the 1923 stable and in this location was reasonably protected from avalanches.

Cole extracted many items of mining and milling equipment from the Brooks-Willis operation: some were reused and others sold to other mining operations. In his years of the lease, Cole, similar to all the others, had huge plans of once again restoring the Jack to what it was.

The Twin Lakes Road from the Tomyhoi trailhead to Twin Lakes, which was somewhat passable by Jeep, was constructed into a driveable road in the summer and fall of 1950. This road was constructed through the 1939 Mine to Market Statute in the State of Washington.

The statute states that if five or more citizens were interested in the development of mineral deposits to be serviced by a road, the group could petition the county commissions of a said county to construct a Mine to Market road. This construction project was completed by the Whatcom County Road Department and was the last year for this Mine to Market Program. In a 1958 publication of Ford Motor Co. called "Ford Times,"an article with pictures of a new 1958 Ford convertible was displayed in the switch back turns below Twin Lakes. The article states that the Twin Lakes road is the state's "shortest road with the mostest."

Lone Jack Blast

In the summer of 1960, while hiking in the surrounding area near Twin Lakes, a Boy Scout Troop investigated the main work adit of the Lulu workings of the Lone Jack. At the end of a side adit, 400 feet in, 400 to 500 boxes of dynamite were discovered. The leader of the troop

129

ordered immediately all the scouts out and, upon returning to Glacier, reported their discovery to the Forest Service. With the leader's strong complaint for public safety, the Forest Service contacted the Washington State Department of Labor, the state agency controlling this type of matter.

Harry Bullene, owner of the mine, of course knew of the dynamite, as did many other people. The dynamite had been placed in the mine in 1925, and had become highly crystallized with a large volume of nitroglycerine seeping down in the cracks of the rock and into the water held within the adit. In October 1963, an attempt to "clean out" the mine failed when the news leaked out and tourists journeyed into the area to observe the fireworks.

On August 30, 1964 with the leadership of a Fort Lewis demolition team, the operation to detonate the dynamite was once again underway. The date of the blast was kept secret. As the caravan of three Army trucks and one Forest Service truck made the climb up Twin Lakes Road, signs were posted closing the area for the day. The total manpower for the day totaled 15 men with a mix of Army and Forest Service personnel, a Bellingham Herald reporter, and Jerry Bourn, who was acting as the guide. Bourn's dad, Charlie, had 40 years earlier packed the problem dynamite by horse to the Jack.

The team carried in an additional 10 cases of dynamite and all equipment as needed to detonate the charge. The Lulu site was already covered with an early August snowstorm, and on this day a heavy snow was falling. The trip in and out was lengthy and difficult for some of the Army boys, as they had never been in the North Cascade Mountains.

The charge was positioned and the personnel moved a safe distance away. The Army experts felt that the setting of the charge could have a major impact on Bear Mountain with the Lulu portal being blown shut by a possible landslide. With the setting of the charge, the blast of air and dust shot out of the Lulu adit and upper vent holes hundreds of feet and then all was quiet.

Allowing the dust to clear, the group entered the adit to discover that the blast had caused no major damage. The room that had stored the dynamite was back where the adit made a couple of turns and the blast destroyed all the work ladder systems and wood ore bulkheads. Also, the blast shot all of the steel pipe and ore cart track into one of the corners, creating a ball of twisted steel that required a worker with a cutting torch days to clear.

The Lone Jack proved what solid rock she was made of, and proved that she will be there for centuries to come. Jerry Bourn was most interested in the blast to learn whether the blast had opened any new quartz veins that would indicate a new gold source. One could only guess that, within a few days, Bourn returned to the Jack for a closer look.

Cache of dynamite in the Lulu adit.
(J. Munroe)

With the death of both Harry and Mamie Bullene, their two children, Elaine Dick and John Bullene, both at that time of Bellingham, inherited all the assets of the Lone Jack.

In the spring of 1965, Robert Cole and an associate, S.A. Collender, were performing exploratory and developmental work on the claims. When the report of the explorations indicated a substantial ore body, the two requested a permit to construct a year-round road to the mine.

The request to the Forest Service was to construct a road from the intersection of the Canadian border and Silesia Creek, following the creek to a point where access to the Lone Jack claim could be made. The requested right-of-way would be used to transport equipment, supplies and construction materials to the mine property. It was their intent to construct a mill on the site with no ore-bearing aggregate being trucked over the proposed roadway. No further correspondence concerning this item was recorded by either side.

In January of 1967 in a report by a mining engineer of the Forest Service, a determination was made that all of the non-patented claims of the Lone Jack proved to be of no mineral value, and also that no yearly assessment work was being performed. All of these claims revoked back to the Forest Service.

Death in Lulu Gulch

Clarence Keplinger and Ben Hinkle, long-time friends, both had a deep love for prospecting in the Cascade Mountains. Keplinger was the principal, besides being the fifth- and-sixth grade teacher at the Maple Falls Grade School (the author had Keplinger for a teacher in the sixth grade). Ben Hinkle was a captain in the Bellingham Fire Department. Keplinger, Hinkle, and a third member spent numerous weekends prospecting in the mountains of the Mount Baker Mining District and in 1967 had established the Dead Goat Claim of molybdenite in the headwaters of the Baker River.

On June 7, 1969, Keplinger and Hinkle started out for a one day prospecting and gold panning trip to Silesia Creek. The Twin Lakes Road, in 1969, was shut off at the Tomyhoi Trail head. Their route was to hike up to Twin Lakes, then around Bear Mountain on the High Trail to Lulu Gulch and then directly down the snowfield to Silesia Creek.

In Lulu Gulch, Hinkle saw a boulder higher up on the snow and set out to investigate. Keplinger turned down and yelled to Hinkle that he planned to stop below a series of lower small cliffs for a lunch break. Within 20 minutes and with Keplinger out of sight, an avalanche of about 4 to 5 dump truck loads of ice blocks broke loose on the top of the ridge of Bear Mountain and came charging down the gulch, missing Hinkle by only 100 feet. With the avalanche heading directly in the direction that Keplinger had taken, Hinkle shouted as loud as possible to warn Keplinger.

Keplinger had served in the military and had suffered severe ear damage. He apparently didn't hear the shout from Hinkle or the avalanche, and was struck with the full force. Keplinger was killed instantly and the removal of his body was by the Whatcom County Sheriff's Office, the Forest Service, and the Bellingham Mountain Rescue (the author was part of this operation). His wife, three daughters, and four sons survived Keplinger.

Calkins Lease

After the Cole lease, established by Josephine Brooks, ran for many years without any return, John Bullene and Elaine Dick terminated the lease and created a new lease in 1975 with Richard Calkins of the Calkins Equipment Co. of Everett. Calkins filed on a new claim, named "Silesia," which had a common border with the north side of the Whist.

Calkins' intent was to construct a flat heliport for his helicopter and to fly sling loads of hand picked ore to Twin Lakes and later to haul it out by commercial dump trucks. Calkins planned to haul out sample loads only

and then, if proven economically sound, to move into full operation. No further action by Calkins was taken.

Anderson Lease

Again with no return to John Bullene and Elaine Dick, the Calkins lease was terminated. In 1979, Tom Anderson, representing a group of partners, signed a new lease with the family. This new mining company was incorporated under the name of Lone Jack Co. in 1980. The Lone Jack Co. was made up of local Whatcom County men with a common commitment to offer their time, money, and equipment with work being performed on weekends and the three months of the summer.

The company's plan of operation for the Lone Jack Mine required that in the first year a six-foot (minimum width) road be constructed from the existing road end (Cole's Road) to the mine. This proposed project would provide the first vehicle road to the mine site after 82 years. Also, the plan called for transporting 30 tons of equipment and supplies to the mine.

With equipment and supplies at the mine site, the new operators planned to: 1) begin mining operations; 2) set up an ore processing mill in the present work tunnel; and 3) set up camp in the unused access tunnel. This camp would be stacked with provisions for startup next spring. The second season they planned to hike to the mine and start operations by mid-May. As soon as the road was free of snow, the road would be opened with yearly maintenance and then necessary

Loading up a charge. (J. Mitchell)

Donkey loaded with gear. (J. Mitchell)

Loading up a series of holes for the road construction looking across Lulu Gulch. (J. Mitchell)

Lone Jack Co. modified two Army Jeeps to become one small dump truck. (J. Mitchell)

equipment changes and improvements would be made. The plan to this point called for removal and processing of 1,000 tons of ore.

However, the first year required the submittal and the approval of a road plan to the Forest Service. The second year and half of the third year was required for the completion of the 6 foot-wide road with transportation of

equipment and supplies to the site. The Lulu adits and stope areas all required days of cleaning out. The installation of air piping, wood ladders and ore hopper was completed.

The Lone Jack Co., having changed its mind about site processing the ore, received word that the smelter in Tacoma agreed to process the ore and immediately a sample was sent.

However, the Tacoma smelter shut down permanently the following spring before any ore could be shipped.

By this time, the energy and resources of this group were nearly expended. Tom Anderson took the need for funding to Vancouver, B.C., and with Canadian investors created a company named "Lone Jack Resources," which appeared on the Vancouver Stock Exchange using the symbol LJR. This Vancouver attempt failed to add the needed funding. The Lone Jack Co. struggled on for three to four years and finally caved in like many of the past. The Jack had won another battle.

Diversified Development Co.

Again, as with past attempts, the Bullenes terminated the lease and moved on. The man to be granted a lease next on July 1, 1984 was S.A. Collender of Langley, Wash., doing business as SAC Co. Inc. and Diversified Development Co.

On Sept. 11, 1984, A. Robert Grant, Inc., a consulting economic geologist, submitted a Report of Evaluation to Delmore Enterprises of British Columbia on the Lone Jack. Delmore Enterprises was to be some level of ownership or a future partner with Collender on the Lone Jack.

The report gave an in-depth review by this qualified consultant. The completed property evaluation, made during the period of Aug. 16-21, 1984, included detailed mapping and sampling of all surface and underground exposures of gold-quartz mineralization. The report covered all three veins, the Lone Jack, the Lulu, and the Whist.

The report states that samples from the Lone Jack ran an average of 2.031 ounces per ton (o/t) of gold. However, the report also indicates that the Lone Jack is basically mined out. The Lulu report states that the average gold is 0.619 o/t with approximately 12,750 tons available in reserve. The Whist is a totally untested target, which has had no previous development. From sampling at the vein, the probable grade range is from 0.5 to 1.0 o/t of gold.

The Grant report recommended that exploration work should be limited to a relatively modest drilling program with a complete plan of location of holes and angle of the holes. Grant estimated the proposed drilling cost at $99,300 (U.S.).

Charles Stone, a mining engineer from Bellingham as indicated in the above Grant report, carried out the drilling program in the fall of 1985. A drilling company from Princeton, B.C. was hired to perform the actual drilling, and two geology students from Western Washington State University were hired as diamond drill helpers.

All the crew and equipment was in place on Oct. 3, 1985, and the drilling work commenced the next day. The crew drilled the recommended hole to the angle as required to a depth of 60 feet, samples were taken from the hole, and no quartz ore-bearing gold was found. The second hole basically brought the same results as the first.

On Oct. 9, 1985, the operation was moved into the old powder magazine. An extremely cold night reversed the airflow in the Lulu adit, resulting in the two-inch PVC airline blowing up and disintegrating. All work was stopped and a worker was dispatched to Bellingham for 400 feet of steel pipe and fittings.

Light snow was falling Oct. 12, 1985, and the decision was made to move out all equipment and men the next day. On the following day, there was 6 inches of new snow and the following day there was 9 more inches. The Lone Jack again was closed for the year. In the Stone report, he stated that in his opinion the Lulu vein had an ore reserve of 5,200 tons and a gold ratio of 0.58 o/t.

In 1986, work was performed on the roadway and general maintenance work was done but the need for capital was of utmost importance. In 1986, there was a story that the Delmore/Collender Group sold its interest to a Vancouver company by the name of Hong Kong Gold. The story proved to be false.

In the early 1990's, Diversified Development found what was needed in a group of area businessmen who were willing to place the needed money into the Lone Jack. This group is comprised of 13 members with a variety of business experience, including a geologist, mining

engineer, a construction equipment man, a logger/road builder, and many others with mixed qualifications. This operation is under the current agreement of Jan. 1, 1990 with the Bullenes. Chris Secrist of Bellingham is secretary. Within a few years, the thirteen members bought out Diversified Development and Bud Collender.

The small-scale mining operation begins each year about Aug. 15 and operates until about Nov. 15. Both the start and finish date are modified yearly by the snow level. The total crew size is three to four men. The gold ore is hauled to Twin Lakes using an Army 6x6 truck and is stockpiled. The stockpiled ore is trucked to Bellingham by a standard 10-yard dump truck and then shipped to any available operating smelter.

In the first season of September 1991, the action of selecting bulk samples and constructing the road up to the Whist vein was performed. The first year that ore was shipped was 1992 and shipments also were made in 1993, 1994, 1995, and 1996. A total of 2,853 tons were shipped with a average of 1.39 o/t or a total of 3,955 ounces of gold shipped.

The 39-percent grade road that had been constructed by the Lone Jack Co. was extremely narrow for moving equipment into the site in 1991. The moving in of a bulldozer was found to be nerve-wracking. The mobile rock drill traveled on the road with the operator supported from a platform mounted on the outside edge of the

Lane Griffin (right) with 6 X 6 Army dump truck used to haul ore from mine site to ore pile site at Twin Lakes. (C. Secrist)

Dump truck at the ore stock pile site. (C. Secrist)

Mucking machine loading 6 X 6 dump truck. (C. Secrist)

Mucking machine used for moving ore and waste material. Note that machine was used to open the portal in the middle of August of snow. (C. Secrist)

John Bullene (left) having a discussion about the operation. (C. Secrist)

Chris Secrist checking the quartz vein. (C. Secrist)

Clair Dalton, the head miner from Prince Edward Island on the East Coast of Canada. (C. Secrist)

Miners riding the lift to the upper adit. (C. Secrist)

Looking straight up at the working stope in the Whist. (C. Secrist)

machine suspended over a 500-foot drop into Lulu Gulch.

The first mining crew arrived from Idaho to work at the site and after the first day the miners returned to Glacier with a couple of the owners to have a few beers. After the Idaho boys had a few beers, they started to express themselves about the Jack. Each stated that it was the most desolate, steepest terrain any of them had ever seen or worked in.

After years of attempting to bring in outside miners, Diversified Development Co. created its own seasonal crew that has been repeatedly used for years. One of the main members of this crew is a stout Canadian hard-rock miner by the name of Clair Dalton. Dalton's farm is on Prince Edward Island on the East Coast of Canada. He is the head miner and performs all of the layout, drilling, and blasting. This man returns each year and takes great pride in developing the Jack.

A few years back, Dalton was the only person in the mine and working in the vertical quartz stope. He suddenly appeared at the mouth of the adit limping and looked a mess. He came up to his fellow worker and in his strong British accent said, "Jon, I took a bit of a nasty tumble." Dalton had fallen about 25 to 30 feet, banging off sidewalls on his way down. He sat down for a few minutes, stood up, dusted himself off, and headed back inside the adit to resume work.

No ore has been shipped to a smelter since 1995, when the price of gold dropped. Then when the price did shoot up to an all-time high, the smelter in Eastern Washington, which was the next planned processor, shut down. They have constructed a second drift lower down to intersect the vein and are ready to continue.

Chapter 8
Last Sourdough

Trip to Bellingham

Officer Dehardt Erickson and a fellow officer received a call from Bellingham Police dispatch concerning an older drunken man who was about to proceed in battle with a group of young men in Dick's Tavern. Upon arriving and entering the tavern, the officers discovered that the man who was about to brawl with the group was a grizzly looking mountain man by the name of Jerry Bourn.

Erickson had an ongoing friendship for years with this man. Erickson had dreamed of being a prospector-mountain man as he spent his free time in the mountains. On many occasions when returning on his way home, he'd stop and visit Jerry, who resided in a true mountain cabin at Shuksan on the Hannegan Pass Road.

Once inside the tavern, the two officers realized Jerry was outnumbered four to one, and the four were longhaired hippie-type fellows of the 1970's. The two patrolmen escorted Jerry to the police car and listened to his version of how the four were provoking him into a confrontation.

Returning to the drinking establishment, the officers quickly figured that Jerry was correct. After they returned to the car, Jerry recognized Erickson and said,

"Erickson, why don't you and me go back in and kick their asses." Erickson stood pondering the request, shook his head and finally slowly said, "I would love to Jerry but I can't."

After discussing the situation, Erickson decided to release Jerry when he promised to proceed home that evening. Jerry told Erickson how he was to be in Bellingham. The previous fall, he had been highgrading (stealing) shake blocks from the Forest Service on the hillside about one-third mile above his Shuksan cabin. He located three or four downed solid cedar trees and had been busy working for a couple of weeks.

After the area received a couple feet of snow, his five dogs were hooked to a sled using an old Chevy hood and the blocks were hauled to the cabin site. These blocks were then loaded onto the truck of an area logger, as Jerry could not have hauled the blocks past the Forest Service Ranger Station in Glacier without being seen. However, with the use of this other truck, the task was done easily.

The blocks were then trucked to a shake mill in Maple Falls and sold for cash. The money was used to purchase a half-ton of dry dog food for his eight dogs for the following year, which was the main reason for the trip to Bellingham. Jerry stated that he had discovered some change remaining after the purchase and was drinking it up. Jerry concluded he was about to head home and the next time Erickson was up in the mountains he should make a point to stop for a cup of coffee.

The following evening, Erickson and his fellow officer were again patrolling Bellingham and received another call to respond to a disturbance at Dick's Tavern. Upon entering the establishment, Jerry was standing upright on the bar about to do battle with a different group. The two officers placed a reluctant Jerry in the patrol car.

Erickson this time was extremely angry with the man and said to him, "Jerry, you said you were heading home, and you didn't go. What is the deal?" Jerry replied, "I found some more money in another pocket, and decided to hang around another day."

Erickson then asked him how he was planning to get home and the answer was that, as always, he would hitch a ride. Erickson said "No, you are going to ride with me until I get off duty, and then I am going to drive you home in this police car."

Charles Bourn Family

Charles and Margaret (Fillman) Bourn were married Oct. 3, 1897, in Wisconsin. Henry Charles Bourn, the father of Charles Bourn, and Jacob Fillman, the father of Margaret (Fillman) Bourn both fought in the Civil War for the Union side. Bourn went through without a scratch.

Pack ready to head out. (G. Byeman)

Pack of Jerry's dogs with Bourn-made harness. (G. Byeman)

Jerry's pack in the middle of Swamp Creek. (G. Byeman)

However, Fillman was wounded at the Battle of Gettysburg.

Charlie finished school in the third grade, but Margaret graduated with a degree as a teacher and had taught in public schools for seven years before the two were married. On Dec. 1, 1898, a girl named Eleanor was born to Margaret, followed by son John then daughter May.

Jacob Fillman had a dislike toward Charlie because Charlie's lack of education, he felt, could hold back Margaret from a good future and life. Also, Charlie developed a serious drinking problem at an early point in the marriage. Margaret with Eleanor left him for a period of time and the family helped to place him in a dry-out program, which was called the Keeley Cure. Charlie left Wisconsin, and traveled to Washington State in search of the location of a timber claim. He first found employment, using a team of horses and wagon, hauling cedar blocks for a shingle mill in Acme.

Margaret traveled west in 1905 on the train to Maple Falls, meeting once again with Charlie where a house was rented in town. Charlie was driving a team with a wagon, again hauling cedar to the Erbb's cedar mill. The Bourn family relocated again to a timber claim on the Nooksack River above the Herman Steiner homestead near Warnick, which was west of Glacier. This timber claim contained 160 acres with a sad state of a residence. Government regulations required that the holder stay five years to prove up and achieve a free title.

While at this home Margaret added two children. The first was a girl who survived only two hours and was buried on the hillside above the house. Next, David Charles was born and he died of spinal meningitis when he was approximately 2 years old.

Charlie's Business Ventures

Following the five-year period of time to prove up, Charlie received ownership of the claim. Charlie sold the timber claim for a large sum of money and relocated the family to Bellingham, where he found some type of new employment.

After a short time in Bellingham, in which Charlie found city life unlivable, the family moved quickly back to the Glacier area. With money from the sale of timberlands, Charlie had funds to purchase two farms in the area, 160 acres of the old Cornell Place on Cornell Creek and then the 80 acres of the old Weggens Place.

Charlie started a new livelihood as a dairy farmer. This new venture quickly grew to 15 cows and the milk was being sold from Maple Falls to Glacier. While on the farms, two additional children were born, the first being Tom in 1909 and two years later Genevieve (Jen).

With the arrival of the railroad in Glacier, Charlie saw another new opportunity. He sold the farms, moved the family back to downtown Glacier and began building the Glacier Hotel, which became the top hotel or boardinghouse with running water and a tennis court. This building was a three-story affair with electric lighting and central heating.

The Bourns built a commodious hotel, but it took the hiring of a couple named Hoxton and Swetmen to set a suitable food table and put out commendable service in 1910 and 1911. In 1911 in Glacier, there was only one other noted hotel, the Mountain Home Hotel that was owned and operated by Mr. and Mrs. Jacobs. After operating for a short period of time, the Glacier Hotel was destroyed by fire for a total loss. From this time forward, Charlie appeared to no longer have any sizeable amount of money so we assume that the hotel had no insurance coverage.

By the time of the hotel fire, the oldest child, Eleanor, had moved to Bremerton, and was employed by the naval shipyard. Seeing the condition of the family finances, Eleanor in the early 1920's purchased the McKenzie's Livery Stable in Glacier for $1,000 for her father to operate. Chet McKenzie opened the Livery Stable and Stage Line in about 1911 and operated it until 1919.

Acquisition of McKenzie's Livery Stable was the best thing that could have happened to Charlie because of his past experience with horses and mules. Quickly, he expanded this business for the needs of tourists, U.S. Forest Service, area mining, the development of the Mt. Baker Highway, and the Mt. Baker Development Co. with the construction of the Mt. Baker Lodge.

After the birth of Gerald Reginald (Jerry) on Dec. 12, 1915, Margaret became seriously ill and was bed ridden. Charlie was forced to hire a full-time nanny to care for the house, Margaret, and all the children. After going though many nannies and much frustration, Charlie placed an ad in the Maple Falls Leader to hire a full-time nanny. Lowella Bell, a young woman and native of Maple Falls who worked as telephone operator for the phone company in Maple Falls, applied and received the job.

Even with Lowella's full health treatment, Margaret's condition continued to decline and she died on May 7, 1920. Charlie then courted the nanny and the two were married. The marriage had 30 years of age difference between the two. From this marriage a daughter, Charlotte, was born.

Included in the purchase of the livery stable, Charlie received the building, all the gear for packing, and all the horses and mules. Charlie, at the peak of the business, had a total of 56 horses. Tom, Jerry, and Lowella all helped Charlie operate the livery stable along with the horses and packing supplies.

The largest need of the operation was that of the mining district, then the Forest Service, survey crews, tourists, and mountain climbers. In the early 1920's all of the surveying, engineering, and layout of the future Mt. Baker Highway, along with the development of the Mt. Baker Lodge, created an enormous undertaking for the area. In the summer, if regional forest fires were underway, Charlie was hired by the Forest Service to pack in the food, supplies, and men. Charlie operated the main pack train to the Lone Jack and in 1925 the Lone Jack crew saw a Bourn pack train going in and out each day.

Charlie established the list below showing the 1920 freight rate for freight in and out of the Lone Jack Mine:

Chas. Bourn, Glacier, Washington
Freight—Shuksan to Lone Jack Mine
By Pony Pack .... 2 cents per lb.
Concentrate on return trip will be some cheaper.

In 1941, the Forest Service had a devastating forest fire that burned the better part of a month and Charlie provided all the packhorses and packers until the fire was extinguished. Charlie Bourn was in his 70's at the time.

Charlie Bourn's pack horses with Birch, the Forest Service Glacier ranger, in the Heather Meadows area in about 1922. Charlie is on the horse. (C. Kvistad)

Large group looking over Heather Meadows—young Tom Bourn sitting on log. (C. Kvistad)

Tom Bourn with work horse at Lone Jack. (B. Peters)

Mountaineer Accidents

C.C. Wright, a climbing guide from Glacier, was leading his only client, J.C. Bishop, a Canadian, on Mt. Baker. They successfully reached the summit but Bishop on the return plunged into a hidden crevasse and died instantly. The date was July 1913. As a result of the fall, Bishop was wedged headfirst into a narrow bottom of the crevasse.

Wright, with night approaching, rapidly returned to Glacier searching for help. In finding that no help could be found either from the Forest Service or the Whatcom County Sheriff's Office, he sought out Charlie Bourn for assistance. Wright hired Charlie with a local high school student and with four horses returned to the site of the accident the following morning.

Leaving the horses at the edge of the glacier, the three hiked to the edge of the crevasse at the site of the accident. Getting to the edge of the crevasse, Wright refused to descend into the crevasse and attach a rope to the body. After attempting to get

Wright to descend, Charlie said, "Oh, what the hell." Charlie was lowered down, tied a second rope to the victim, and then both were pulled to the surface. Bishop's body was lowered down the glacier surface to the horses, loaded, and then the group returned to Glacier. That was Charlie's only true mountain-climbing experience.

When a sudden and major avalanche on Mt. Baker killed six college students from Western Washington State College on July 22, 1939, Charlie's pack train was once more called to service. This climbing party included 25 climbers with two veteran guides.

When the word of the worst climbing accident in history on Mt. Baker reached Glacier, Charlie realized the immediate up-coming need for packhorses and went to preparing the pack trains. As he was doing this, all the residents of Glacier gathered and prepared food supplies to be shipped in on the first trip up. The horses were to travel the Glacier Creek Trail to Kulshan Cabin and then continue up as high as the snow level on Heliotrope Ridge.

With many people gathering in Glacier for information, a reporter arrived in Glacier from the Seattle Post-Intelligencer and went directly to Charlie with a request to hire a guide and horse to visit the accident site. Charlie, knowing that all of his packers were all on the trail, said "Sure, you be ready to go in one hour."

Charlie went looking for his daughter Charlotte, who was 12 or 13 at the time. After being told of her first guiding trip, Charlotte said that she had not been up that trail and was told by her father, "You will do fine. All you need to do is follow the horse tracks and manure." The shocked reporter stood with his mouth open as the young girl arrived with the horses, but he had no other choice. The trip up to the snow line was uneventful, and after depositing the reporter at snow level, Charlotte turned and headed down.

Seeing one of her father's earlier pack trains, she joined it and started back to town. The horse ahead carried one of the dead climbers tied over its back. The impact of this sight did not affect Charlotte at the time because she was trying to act mature for her age, but later in the days to follow this sight remained in her thoughts.

Horse Camps

Charlie constructed two horse camps with one located on the Hannegan Pass Road, about 100 yards from the Mt. Baker Highway (where the road makes the hard left turn and the spot where the picnic table with a toilet are presently located). The second is up the Twin Lakes Trail at the start of the Tomyhoi Lake Trail. Each of these camps had a rail corral for the animals, a roofed area for hay storage, and a lean-to structure that provided shelter and sleeping area for five to six men.

In the busy summer time, Charlie housed the horses and men at one or both of these two base camps if they were not out in the backcountry. The bulk of all the needed services centered from these two locations. Tom and Jerry, the two youngest Bourn boys, constantly traveled on horse trips with Dad when not in school with Jerry riding behind Charlie and Tom walking.

With Charlie having the horse camp on the Hannegan Pass Road, his old friend Charlie Anderson staked five mining claims where Swamp Creek entered the Nooksack River. The No. 1 claim was the lowest one, located at the river level. Immediately, Anderson set to constructing a permanent cabin on the site and Charlie Bourn, in passing the site, would volunteer his 13-year-old son Jerry to assist in the construction. Jerry's stay could have been for the day or in some cases for a week, depending when Dad returned. This cabin, in later years, became known as the "Jerry Bourn Cabin."

Tom & Jerry's Upbringing

With all the activity in mining surrounding Glacier, Tom and Jerry Bourn, in their growing-up years, were exposed to a community that was deeply involved in mining. It's not surprising the two became so interested in mining and made it their lifelong main interest. In the early years, Glacier was over-flowing with burned-out miners with no new rush to follow. Many of these old sourdoughs were left over from the Klondike Rush and other rushes throughout the world. The Mt. Baker Rush was one of the last, so Glacier was to become the last home to many.

Amos Zimmer with Jerry Bourn 1940.
(C. Kvistad)

While Tom and Jerry Bourn were raised in Glacier, old miners — including Amos Zimmer, Bert Lowry, Charlie Anderson, Jack Post, Russ Lambert, and many others who are forgotten to history — were in the area. In the Graham Store or the McDonald's Store, each with a large pot-belly stove, these worn-out mining men gathered and discussed daily all the gold yet to be discovered in the local mountains. The two young men were taken into operating mines such as the Lone Jack, Gargett Bros., and Boundary Red with Dad and viewed first hand the different operations. They were taken into the ore mill to see gold being extracted from the ore or into the mine to witness the gold suspended in the quartz vein. With this education, and the field trips with these old sourdoughs along with the trips with their father, these two young brothers were determined to have a life of mining.

Tom Bourn

Tom Bourn, after graduating from the Glacier High School, found employment mainly as a logger or sawmill worker. When given the opportunity, he headed to the mountains for prospecting or mining. Another of Tom's skills was that of an experienced trapper/hunter, again with proficiency gained from the old timers of Glacier.

Tom established trap lines originating at Glacier with the main line up Canyon Creek. One summer, Tom pioneered a trail up the creek, which required building shelters spaced about two or three miles apart. When winter arrived, he would head up the creek on snowshoes to Damifino Lakes, disappearing for weeks. Tom pioneered the route up the creek for the future trail that was completed by Civilian Conservation Corps workers. Tom labored at many of the district mines such as the Lone Jack, Gargett Bros., and the Boundary Red.

Tom's principal interest in local mining focused on the Boundary Red Mountain Mine, located on the northeast face of Red Mountain and perched directly above Silesia Creek and Canada. The U.S. route to the Red follows the trail to Twin Lakes, down Silesia Creek and directly up to the mine above the border. The preferred route, that being the Canadian route, went up the Chilliwack River to a location directly beneath the mine, followed by an ascent up the precipitous hillside. The Boundary

Red Mine location was every bit as steep of terrain as the Lone Jack and in some cases more inaccessible.

Tom Braithwaite and C.W. Both discovered the Boundary Red Mine while on a mountain goat hunting excursion in the region in 1897. The claim changed hands in 1902 and development started at a moderate pace.

The Red is located similar to the Jack at a high elevation (4,050 feet) on the north side of Red Mountain, and the winter snow lay on the ground until later in the summer or early fall. In long winter years with heavy snowfalls, the snow directly above the mine remains year-round with a threat of avalanche danger.

The Boundary Red was established as a chief producer and a profitable gold mine that operated for years with a modern milling operation and living quarters for the personnel. The Boundary Red also received the distinction of being the wettest mine operation in Washington State. The water problem decreased in the winter due to the lack of melting snow and all the surface water freezing.

Due to this water problem, the Red had also the designation of having three crews: the first is an incoming crew to work, the next actually working, and the third leaving. The Red's main problem was maintaining a crew. The Boundary Red initiated operation in 1914 and operated intermittently until 1938.

Tom Bourn and W.W. Wagner in 1939, purchased the mine in receivership from a local bank for $12,000. This purchase required the life-long savings Tom had acquired, however, he felt strongly that there was wealth to come out of the old girl yet. The two long-time friends built improvements at the mine with a one or two-man crew. They added a sawmill and rod mill, and improved the living quarters in preparation of restarting.

In 1941, the United States became involved in World War II and the draft placed Tom into military service. Upon returning following the war, he again placed all of his energy in the Red in preparation for a long-delayed restart.

In the late spring of 1944 or 1945, Tom hiked up to review preparation for the year's operation. Upon his quick return from the mine, he went directly to his sister Charlotte in Bellingham and told her with tears in his eyes of an enormous avalanche that swept down Red Mountain and completely destroyed all of the mill buildings. The following day, Tom could stand it no longer and set out to return to the mine to reassess the damage. In the elapsed time between his descent and return, he discovered that a second and larger avalanche had roared down the mountain face, destroying the cookhouse and bunkhouse.

Following the second trip, Tom returned to Charlotte's home and this time he appeared to be a totally shaken man. When he viewed the first avalanche, he was planning to remain in the bunkhouse, but changed his mind and came out. If he had remained, Tom felt the second slide surely would have killed him.

With this disappointment, Tom relocated to the southern part of the state and owned and operated a small sawmill with a rock quarry for the remainder of his life. Because of the loss of the Red, Tom never searched for gold again.

The Boundary Red Mine is situated on patented claims such as the Lone Jack. Following the disaster that destroyed all of the operation, Tom Bourn remained with clear title of the property until his death. Tom met a young geologist/miner in the mountains while prospecting by the name of Tom Wiatrak, who was from a wealthy family in Seattle. The two men became close friends while making many prospecting trips together. At one point, they traveled down to Mexico for an extended trip of prospecting. At the time of his death, Tom willed the Red to Tom Wiatrak, and the Red remains presently in the ownership of the Wiatrak family.

Young Jerry Bourn

Jerry Bourn attended Glacier School District for grade school and later transferred to the Maple Falls High School after Glacier School District was consolidated with the Maple Falls School District. Jerry, being an above-average student, placed first in a countywide essay writing contest in the fifth or sixth grade. In high school, he again placed first in a county debate contest. Many of the Bourn family felt that if Jerry's mother had lived and with her teaching ability Jerry may have discovered a future in higher education. Jerry, with an intense interest in helping his father doctor horses at a young age, may have gone on to a future in medicine. Jerry graduated from high school in 1934.

In later life when he lived at Shuksan, Jerry listened to a battery operated radio and knew locations up on the hillside where he could listen to stations with world news. Jerry was dedicated to the weekly radio program called The World Tomorrow with Garner Ted Armstrong. If you, as a friend, a relative, or a beautiful woman were present, you were told by Jerry that all conversation must stop for the half-hour. With all the visitors to the cabin, he asked them to bring any used newspaper.

Jerry, after school, was similar to other young men of the area and worked in the logging industry. Jerry's qualifications included timber faller, equipment operator, and high rigger. When a parcel of timber needed harvesting near the power line which ran from the Excelsior Power Plant to Glacier and no other timber cutters would attempt it, Jerry took the challenging job. Not one time throughout this cutting and harvesting project did the lights flicker in Glacier.

A high rigger employed up the Swamp Creek Road was cutting the top out of a tree for a future spar tree when he accidentally, at approximately 120 feet up, cut his climbing belt safety rope with his axe and fell to his death. In a few days, the foreman for the logging company tried to locate another high rigger to climb the tree and complete the job. No one would go up because they all felt that the tree was now haunted.

The foreman drove down to Glacier, found Jerry, and asked if he would finish the job. Jerry answered, "Oh what the hell, sure," went up and completed the tree. Jerry was employed in the logging industry in the winter and spring but in late summer and the fall he departed to the mountains to prospect.

A real highlight in Jerry's young adult life occurred in 1935 with the filming of the Hollywood movie of Jack London's "Call of the Wild" on the slopes and foothills of Mt. Baker. Directly in front of the Anderson Cabin (later Bourn Cabin), a scene was shot with Shuksan in the background and canoes with Indians on the river. The canoes accidentally capsized in the river and all the Indians were saved but all of their gear was lost. Later, Jerry recovered their arrows down-stream and to his dying day they were displayed in the cabin. Jerry along with many other locals were employed by the movie as extras. Jerry recalls, "We made good money that time. Five dollars apiece per day."

The threesome—Tom Bourn, Tom Waggor, and Jerry—were constantly in the mountains in search of the big strike. Tom Waggor had a cousin named Betty O'Brien who was a nurse in Medford, Ore. Jerry, following a short courtship, married her. Jerry and Betty lived in Oregon with Jerry employed as a logger or similar jobs.

Jerry's Army Career

In 1941 with the United States being drawn into World War II, Jerry enlisted in the Army. While Jerry was overseas, Jerry and Betty adopted a newly born boy, who was named Dennis Larry Bourn. While Jerry was in the service, he received like many others a "Dear Jerry letter." This unfortunate event was of one of many that was to shape his life in years to follow.

Jerry trained with thousands of other Army GIs for the invasion of Kiska Island in the Aleutian Islands in Alaska. This was intended to be a major conflict. However, on the invasion date of Aug. 14, 1943, they discovered that the Japanese had completely fled off the Island under the screen of weeklong fog. The U.S. Army advanced ashore with the majority of the soldiers ready to face combat in what was anticipated to be one of the bloodiest of the war.

As the Army settled at the abandoned Japanese Camp, a few days later one lone Japanese soldier who must have been left behind was discovered. This Japanese soldier repeatedly was seen at night searching through the garbage dump for food.

The question of what to do with this fellow became a topic of hot discussion. The larger group wanted to shoot him, a smaller group wanted to take him prisoner, and the smallest group wanted to let him be—to come and live in the camp and assist with chores.

Jerry was strongly in favor with the smallest group, who finally won out and the man was relocated into the camp. Finally, a commanding officer discovered the Japanese houseboy and placed him in a U.S. prison camp off the island. This fellow strongly wished not to go to a prison because following the war he would be returned to Japan. By Japanese custom, he was required to die either in combat or by suicide, and to be taken as a prisoner would be classified as a disgrace.

After leaving Alaska, Jerry's group further trained for jungle warfare for the upcoming invasion of Okinawa. After months of training, they were shipped out again in anticipation of a major battle. However, by the time they reached Okinawa, the invasion and the war were over. With these actions, Jerry's military service was complete and he retired with a master sergeant rank.

Return to Glacier

Jerry returned to Glacier following the war as a single man. Betty, his former wife, had remarried and lived the remainder of her life in Oregon. Many of Jerry's siblings confirmed that Jerry returned an altered man, with a broken spirit, much looser manner, and definitely more of a drinker. Jerry, similar to most men his age who were single and returning from the war, found drinking and partying a major factor in one's life.

Upon his return, Jerry received word that one of fondest old friends had died. Charlie Anderson, the old miner whom Jerry had helped build the Shuksan Cabin, had passed away. Anderson, while Jerry was at war, became a feeble elderly man and repeatedly had fallen sick. The Bourn family moved him down to their residence in Glacier from Shuksan to nurse him back to health. Finally, after years of struggling at his cabin, he relocated into an abandoned cabin on the Bottiger farm near where the Bourn farm had been.

The Bottiger family was similar to the Bourn family in that they were early settlers in Glacier. The family had two sons about the age of Jerry. After a short period of time, Charlie Anderson died. The Bottiger family let it be known that the Shuksan Cabin and all five of the mining claims belonged now to the Bottiger family. In hearing the news, Jerry felt extremely upset due to his fondness of the man and all the work he had performed in the construction of the cabin, but he kept his feelings and thoughts to himself.

Anyone has the right to own mining claims but one item that must be completed is the yearly assessment work. This assessment work is of a required dollar amount and must be reported to the county assessor's office each year in a written report. Jerry laid back and waited patiently for the Bottiger's to neglect the reporting requirement. In a few weeks following the dead-line, Jerry filed on the claims.

In a short period of time, the Bottigers discovered their error and Jerry's filing, which was followed by heated words between the two families. In a month or two, one of the Bottiger sons came forward to say, "Jerry, you better look out because I'm going to shoot you." Jerry stated, "Come forward, it is my cabin now." Nothing ever happened between the two parties and the cabin remained Jerry's until the time of his death.

Winter Mining Project

Tom and Jerry Bourn secretly decided to undertake a winter mining project. The Brooks family of Portland, in the late 1930's, owned the Lone Jack Mine and the Jack had been inactive for years. At the Lone Jack, which ceased operation in 1907, the large mined-out area that is called the stope had ore pillars remaining in place to provide support and keep the ceiling from collapsing. Federal law and common mining procedure required this practice and miners would leave a two to three-foot round rock pillar or bring in wood members to be placed for the support.

The Bourn brothers did not know or maybe did not care who had ownership of the mine. The two hiked in with packhorses loaded with all the needed winter supplies and mining equipment and constructed a camp in the old work adit. They made one trip out to return the horses, then the brothers hiked to the remote Jack for the winter. We must assume that the brothers chose to perform the work in mid-winter because of the need for privacy of their actions. In the stope area, the vein, which is formed of quartz and gold, runs directly through these existing pillars.

The Bourn brothers—remained all winter in the Jack, mining the pillars from the 24 to 30 inch-high stope work area, transporting the ore to the ore dump, and dropping the ore to the haulage tunnel. Near the portal of the adit and their camp, the hand crushing of the ore took place, and then they extracted the gold by panning or mercury.

The brothers, knowing the danger of the ceiling collapsing because of their years in mining, felt sufficiently safe regardless. When the time approached to leave in the spring, the two removed all evidence of their actions, and the brothers journeyed out with their treasure.

Harry Bullene, owner of the Jack in the 1950's and 1960's, traveled to the mine to show his 14 year-old son John all the known property corners and other features of the property. Harry felt that this might be his last opportunity to pass on the information to his son, as he was getting up in years and his health was beginning to fail.

John took in the available information as Harry had repeatedly told him and his sister—with a smile on his face—that some day they would be the proud owners of the Jack. Harry showed John the location of the surface vein as it continued up to the south beyond the discovery point and both easily detected the gold flecks in quartz.

Years later after Harry had passed away, John returned to view this vein and display it to his hunting friends. In finding the location, John was shocked to discover that the vein had been mined out the full height (18 inches) and as far as a person could reach in. John had a suspicion who the thief may be and within a few months paid Jerry a visit. When questioned concerning the matter, Jerry answered looking straight into John's eyes: "Yes, I did it, so." Jerry paused a second or two and than added, "John, how about a cup of coffee?" John left with his answer and nothing of the lost treasure.

Drinking Problem

Jerry's drinking problem worsened and certainly impacted his life. Jerry, similar to some other hard-living loggers in the region, performed his daily work in a somewhat intoxicated state, and the potential damage to himself and others becoming a safety factor.

An emergency telephone call received by the Whatcom County Sheriff's Office indicated that a man was lying on the Mt. Baker Highway east of Glacier. Upon locating the man, the officer identified Jerry Bourn. Down crawling on hands and knees, Jerry was heading up the road following the center paint stripe.

Asked what he was doing, Jerry replied that he was heading home by following the paint stripe so he could find his way.

The officer directed Jerry to climb in the car so he could transport him home. Jerry looked up at him and answered, "Like hell I will. You will get me in the car and then throw my sorry ass in jail." After a half-hour of negotiating, Jerry reluctantly agreed, and was given another of his many free rides home.

Jerry soon thereafter was placed in the Kitsap Alcoholic Rehabilitation Center in Port Orchard with the assistance of his siblings and his position as a veteran. After two weeks, his sister Eleanor and his ex-wife went to see him at the center. Jerry especially enjoyed the center and the girls' visit. He had complete access to the facilities with his own key and he displayed the doctor offices, his room, the meeting rooms, and kitchen, where he prepared them a lunch. As in all instances when he was sober, he was one of most trusted and popular fellows there. After the required completion time, Jerry returned to Glacier and, similar to the majority of others who return to the old lifestyle, he returned to partying with the boys.

The Night of Feb. 26, 1956

One of the lowest points in the life of Jerry Bourn and also in the lives of many others living in the upper Nooksack River Valley occurred on Feb. 26, 1956. Jerry and his friend Nell Nims resided in a small cabin on the site of the Miller Shingle Mill located two miles down river from Glacier. Similar to the other loggers in the area, Jerry was temporarily laid off— "drawing rockin chair," as they called it—caused by the lingering heavy snowfall in the mountains.

On this Sunday, Jerry accompanied by Nell and others, who included Jerry's friend Joe Straka, maintained a complete afternoon and evening of partying. Joe Straka and Jerry were friends their whole life as each was raised in the upper river valley. A few years earlier, Straka's house burned down and the family escaped unhurt, but all of their personal items including clothing were destroyed. Jerry and other friends of the Straka family searched for clothing for the family. Jerry made the rounds of all his friends and included a trip to Bellingham to his sister Charlotte's home, and then delivered the items to Straka's. Jerry, being two years older, graduated from Maple Falls High School ahead of Straka.

The size of gathering reduced down to Jerry, Nell, and Straka with frequent trips between the Bourn house and taverns in Glacier. Back at the Bourn house, an argument broke out and a three-way fight occurred. Straka was hit over the head by Jerry or Nell with Straka's rifle, which had been left there earlier. Nell immediately traveled in the snow by foot to a neighbor who lived about two miles away for assistance. Jerry, in a drunken stupor, passed out on the bed. Joe Straka passed away in a Bellingham hospital the following morning. Jerry was arrested and

placed in Whatcom County Jail facing a charge of first-degree murder. A wife and three young children survived Straka.

Apparently a disturbance in early morning erupted between the two when Straka demanded that Nell prepare him some "scrambled eggs," at which time Jerry said "no and you go home." The argument intensified with the start of a fistfight leading to Straka being struck with the butt of the rifle stock. The prosecuting attorney rested the state's case following the first day of the trial on May 23, 1956. On the following day, Superior Court Judge Bert Kale dismissed the first-degree murder charge, replacing it with a second-degree charge.

Charlie Anderson cabin on Swamp Creek. (J. Steiner)

Bourn cabin deep in winter. (G. Byeman)

On May 25, the case was given to jury for deliberation and on May 27 the eight men and four women of the jury determined Jerry Bourn was innocent of second-degree murder.

The Anderson Cabin

After saying farewell to his latest friends of the jail, inmates and workers alike, Jerry was released from Whatcom County Jail and returned to Glacier and the mountains. Following his release, Jerry and Nell packed up their belongings and relocated up river at the Charlie Anderson cabin at Shuksan. This cabin provided the permanent resident for Jerry the remainder of his life, other than extended prospecting trips, occasional trips to the county jail or to visit with relatives.

Jerry Bourn at his cabin (Charlie Anderson Cabin) on Swamp Creek. (Whatcom Museum)

The cabin is a two-story structure with the surrounding land partly cleared. It is situated on a mining claim, but the land was not owned as a patented claim such as the Lone Jack. The cabin, of course, had no power, water, or indoor toilet facility.

Jerry's rock ledge garden. (J. Steiner)

However, Jerry created numerous mechanical items that improved his lifestyle. He rigged a lightweight steel cable to a rock in the middle of the Nooksack River directly in front of the cabin. It acted similar to a backyard clothesline. With a connection device on the cable to which he could fix a weighted, watertight container, Jerry placed his perishable food. By pulling in the cable, he could remove food from the "refrigerator" and then return it to the river. Also, Jerry created a garden on a rock ledge on the cliff-

face near the road. Water was piped from a nearby stream and, with the heat created on the rock face, he produced a grand vegetable source.

Located directly behind Jerry's cabin is a swampy lake area that existed when Jerry settled in. Jerry borrowed a D7 dozer from his off-and-on old friend Lec Bottiger to enlarge and dam up the stream that passed through the swamp. Jerry built a dam and a control gate. This was to become his private fish farm. Jerry would catch the rainbow trout in the Nooksack River compliments of the State of Washington and release them in the pond. In Jerry's mind, this was his private pond and he ordered with harsh words many fishermen out over the years.

Jerry's method of fishing was to remove the stop gate and drain the water. The pond drained almost totally and then with boots Jerry picked up as many fish as he wanted for dinner. The Forest Service was extremely upset with the construction of the pond and the working of the equipment in the water and equally upset when he pulled the stop gate and flooded all of the lower land. They repeatedly threatened him for this method of fishing but to no avail.

The Forest Service created a policy which stated that in different areas within the National Forest there were to be recreational lots that could be leased for a short term to the general public. In the Glacier District there were two such areas. One of the areas was around the northwest end of the "Jerry Pond." The access road to this area was off the Twin Lakes Road.

The Forest Service created a few leases, and a person, making preparations for the construction of a summer cabin, arrived one Saturday morning to find that "Jerry's Pond" was almost completely dry as Jerry had opened the gate and drained the pond. The irritated man dashed to the district ranger's house in Glacier, and was told by the ranger that the matter would be straightened out on Monday. In talking to Jerry, Jerry informed the ranger that the end of the pond was situated on his mining claim and thus he had complete control over the outlet end. After arguing for over two hours, the ranger threw his arms in the air. With his suggestion, the Forest Service pulled that lease and the others that had been issued.

The two-story, 20 foot x 22 foot cabin, which was Jerry's home for approximately 20 years, had numerous unique items of interest. There were always goat and bear rugs, deer and goat antlers, and the skull, which was a human head, that Jerry claimed was from a past wife. This skull could have been that of one of many men who had disappeared in the mountains or that of the man who was murdered in the Lone Jack. The Whatcom County Sheriff's Office became interested. Upon reviewing the skull and following a conversation with Jerry, the Sheriff's Office determined the skull was that of a Native American and that Jerry located it while digging in a streambed.

The interior of the cabin was very dark with the back two sides of the structure set under huge cedar trees. Also, as stated earlier, there was no electric power. The view of Mt. Shuksan through the front window was breathtakingly fabulous.

The artifacts in the crowded cabin, which Jerry had collected, were items such as mining equipment, traps, hubcaps, and hunting/fishing gear. The front and side walls had shelves that

Jerry on his way to go hunting. (R. Kramer)

held numerous ore samples. Dangling from the walls and ceiling rafters were many items, the results of years of collecting. Every nook and cranny was stuffed with some treasure and laden with dust.

The second floor of the cabin was used for sleeping and storage. Jerry's guest-book, which all visitors were asked to sign, sat on the back corner of the table. Jerry's cabin was always open to strangers when he was home, and his coffee was royal grade with coffee grounds poured directly into the pot and boiled all day. Jerry's white deer (mountain goat) stew, which cooked for one or two days, was the gourmet treat for invited dinner guests. Canning all of his own vegetables was a yearly ritual but his main canning project was that of venison.

Jerry's Animals

Jerry's dogs, which at times totaled as many as eight, were used as pack dogs, and guards, but mainly as companions. The leader of the pack, a female that was a cross between a shepherd and wolf named Lady, was the mother to most of the others. The names of the dogs commonly used were Champ, Shuksan, Grizzly, and Thunder. In the cleared flat in front of the cabin, each dog had his individual doghouse and chain.

Lady, as the leader of the pack, had her house and a dog run crossing the driveway in front of the cabin. She guarded the cabin and no one entered the cabin without passing her. These dogs were all one-man dogs, and to most visitors they appeared to be extremely vicious. No visitor released his pets at Jerry's place for they would have been killed in seconds. Occasionally, an eight-dog fight broke out, usually started over food. Jerry found shooting his rifle to be the only method to halt the fight.

These dogs were used as pack dogs and packed into the mountains regularly with the horse Tony and all the supplies required for an extended expedition. Early in the year on the

Jerry's pack of dogs with Shuksan in the background. (T. Brown)

snow, the dogs were superior to the horse as the dogs could easily cross steep snowfields. All of the dogs had his or her individual pack, fabricated by Jerry out of old surplus canvas, and hand-sewed. The packs were custom-made to fit each dog and these packs all had each dog's name hand-painted on it.

These dogs were born to mountain travel and would go any place that Jerry traveled in the mountains. Jerry had the ability to travel in the dead of night on crude trails with little light and the help of Lady. He told a friend that one system he used to return from down in Silesia Creek to the Shuksan

Four of the dogs on their houses. (G. Byeman)

Jerry on the Silesia Creek Trail having a break. Each dog had it's own pack made by Jerry with its name painted on it. Also note the rifle leaning against the pack with all the tape holding it together. (G. Byeman)

Cabin in the dead of night was to tie a short piece of reflective tape on Lady's tail. Then, a short rope was tied to her neck and with a command from him, "HOME," they would head out for an all-night hike.

One late summer day, Jerry and an employee of the Forest Service were hiking through Twin Lakes Pass to Silesia Creek and paused in the pass for a mouthful to eat and drink. The Forest Service man, as he ate, threw parts of remaining sandwiches in front of the two dogs of Jerry's, but they only continued to sit and glanced at the food.

After being there a short period of time, three other hikers joined them. A woman in the group asked Jerry if she might pet one of his dogs. Jerry answered that the last man who attempted had his hand bit off at the wrist. The woman suddenly stepped backward a few steps and asked Jerry if she could take his picture with the dogs. He answered, "Yes, for $5." She dug into a pouch, gave the $5, then took the picture, said thanks, and the group headed down the trail.

The Forest Service man glanced at a smiling Jerry and asked, "Why had the dogs not eaten the food on the ground." Jerry then looked at the dogs, gave them some type of command, and the dogs jumped into action, devouring the bread in a flash.

In the 1960's, Jerry needed transportation to the Canadian trailhead that led up Silesia Creek and then continued to his Red Lead Mining

Claim. Jerry inquired of numerous friends in Glacier for the excursion and all turned him down or were too busy. Ultimately, Jerry's nephew, Tom Brown, and his wife volunteered for the drive. Tom had recently purchased a nice new car and insisted that the three dogs be hauled in the trunk, not in the backseat as Jerry demanded.

With fully loaded packs on, the dogs were loaded in the trunk, crammed down, and the lid slammed shut. All the way to the Sumas border crossing, the occupants of the car heard the dogs growling at each other. When they arrived at the border, the border agent asked where they were headed and was satisfied with the answer.

When he ordered Tom to open the trunk for inspection, Tom glanced at Jerry, who shook his head. Tom then informed the agent that probably that was not a good idea and told the agent of the trunk full of dogs. When asked how many dogs, Jerry answered and presented the agent the papers for the dogs. The papers were for some dogs but surely not for these dogs. The agent demanded that the trunk be opened and Jerry reluctantly told the agent to proceed with the trunk. The agent, expecting to find anything other than dogs, turned to the rear of the car and opened it. The moment the trunk was thrown open, all three dogs immediately were at a standing position and growling. Suddenly, the agent slammed the trunk, and commanded them to "get the hell going."

René Dove and his 3-year-old son Mike, returning from a day of skiing at the lodge, decided to stop and meet Jerry. René slowly got out of the car, leaving the door ajar for a hasty retreat after the greeting of a growling huge dog on steel cable.

All of a sudden René heard a gruff-sounding man shout at Lady to "shut up" and he then added, "Don't move an inch, I got you covered." This was the standard greeting that Jerry welcomed all unknown or unwelcome visitors.

René answered that he wished to discuss a common friend. Jerry shouted again to Lady and told René to come forward. René entered the cabin and detected the odor of Jerry baking bread. The two discussed the mutual friend for 10-15 minutes with Lady barking the whole time. All of a sudden, René and Jerry realized that the dog had quit barking. René suddenly recalled that his small son was in the car with the door open. Jerry and René bolted through the door to discover that Mike was in fact out of the car, had gone up to Lady, and sat down on the ground. Now Lady had placed her head on Mike's leg and Lady was sound asleep.

Another time when René and his son Mike, who was then 4 years old, were driving through Glacier, they saw some type of incident taking place at the entrance of Graham's Store with a sheriff's car and two deputies nearby. Walking back and forth on the porch of the store were three of Jerry's dogs that were scaring every passerby and the sheriff had been called. However, the deputies, like the others, did not approach the growling dogs. No one seemed to know where Jerry was; they had enough problems with the dogs.

René parked the van across the highway and directed young Mike to go fetch the dogs as he opened the back doors. To the amazement of all the people present, this small 4-year-old boy went to each of the dogs, led them and loaded them into the van. Driving the dogs home, René and Mike could not locate Jerry. They then returned to Glacier to find a drunk Jerry and generously hauled him home.

Jerry had a few different horses at the Shuksan Cabin. The main horse that he had for years was a one-eyed horse named Tony. Tony acted similar to the dogs in that he would follow Jerry in the woods wherever he went. The horse would not require any type of lead. One of the Glacier "want-to-be" miners hiked down to Silesia Creek with Jerry and Tony loaded with gear to operate a sluice box on one of Jerry's many claims. When the party reached the site, Jerry pointed out the area that comprised the claim.

Busy working for a few days, all of a sudden Jerry yelled to his helper to listen. They heard oncoming voices of approaching men. Jerry shouted to his helper, "Run like hell—I'll see you at my cabin." Within a couple miles and almost back to Twin Lakes, the two

met and stopped to rest. After being asked concerning the claim, Jerry answered, "Well actually the claim is not mine and never was." When they got back to the cabin, the helper worried about Tony and questioned Jerry, who reassured him that he would return home in a few days, which he did.

One of many sources of food for the dogs was road killed animals; many were found between the cabin and Glacier. Once Jerry and his friend Nell were in Glacier at Graham's Store drinking a few. A tourist stopped at the grocery store part of the building, telling the store operator that he had accidentally killed a deer. They had loaded the deer in the back of their pickup. After calling the state game department, they were instructed to leave the deer on the front steps of the store and an agent would dispose of the body. The people with the damaged pickup did as advised and headed out of town.

Jerry and Nell came out in a little tipsy mood. Upon seeing the deer Jerry said, "Oh great, a venison dinner for the dogs." With that Jerry and Nell loaded the deer and headed to Shuksan. The only problem with the venison dinner was that some of the local people of Glacier had seen the deer leave town. Upon being questioned by the agent, they told him of Jerry.

The game agent arrived at Jerry's cabin as he was cutting up the animal. Jerry was not too eager to accept the ticket. As the day of the trial arrived, Jerry hitched a ride to Bellingham. Upon getting there early, he found his route to the old watering hole Dick's to steady his nerves.

The judge read the charge of possession of game out of season without a hunting license. When asked how he pleaded, Jerry pleaded guilty and explained that he was only taking the road kill to feed his dogs. The judge listened for a minute or two, then said, "Yes, Mr. Bourn, you are gaining a long record here in the Whatcom County Courthouse. You are guilty, and I fine you $200 payable now."

"Your honor," Jerry pleaded, "I cannot pay $200. I'm not able to pay until I work my gold mine in the summer." "All right I will reduce it $50 and I never want to see you in this courtroom again," the judge replied. "And also, have you been drinking?" "I had one to steady my nerves." Jerry paid the $50 and headed to Glacier.

Tony's barn, located in the flat in front of Jerry's cabin, was built into the backside of a large burned-out cedar stump with a roof of hand-split cedar shakes, compliments of the Forest Service. Jerry gave intensive care to the dogs and horse following the early training of his father. If Jerry saw that the dogs were catching an epidemic case of fleas, he'd take Tony's horse powder and mix it with the dog food. Jerry said it performed two things; first it cleaned the dogs out and secondly them of the fleas.

Two students of horse shoeing watching Tony, Jerry's one-eyed horse, getting fitted. (G. Byeman)

For many years, it surely was a sight to encounter Jerry traveling on Tony with the pack of dogs barking and running up or down a trail. The Forest Service's Silver Fir Campground is across the river near Jerry's cabin. One weekend day in the middle of the camping season with the campground full of kids and pets, Jerry came galloping through the campground full speed on old Tony with his old 30-30 across his lap. With him was his pack of dogs barking and growling at everybody and every dog they could observe. As expected, many of the frightened campers picked up their camps and immediately charged down to the Forest Service office in Glacier to report the terrible incident.

The Forest Service with the Whatcom County Sheriff's Office went to investigate the matter but could not find Jerry. Some of the people thought that the wild man riding through the campground was a staged performance by the Forest Service.

Jerry Bourn Versus United States Government

Jerry Bourn had ongoing conflicts with different government agencies, but the agency that provided the longest continuous battle was the U.S. Forest Service. In its archives in Sedro Woolley, one of the thickest files is the one labeled Jerry Bourn. The Forest Service attempted, over a period of 30 years, to remove Jerry from his mining claims at the cabin site but was not successful. On May 9, 1950, the Forest Service forwarded to Jerry a letter requesting him to relocate from the site because the claim and cabin were within the Forest Service Power Site Classification No. 126. One of the problems for the Forest Service in communicating with Jerry was that he had no permanent address, which then required using general delivery Glacier, and at times his mail would go unopened for months. Jerry ignored this 1950 request similar to others and life went on for both sides.

In a report dated May 6, 1965, the Forest Service stated that Jerry moved into the cabin in 1949 and had lived there ever since. (This is not correct because in the 1950's he was living at the Miller Mill site.) It stated that the cabin was 16 x 20 feet and Jerry had added a barn for his two horses and had added eight dog houses. The report stated there were four mining claims at the site: Shuksan No. 1, where the cabin is situated, Shuksan No. 2, Shuksan No. 3 and the Black Lady.

When requested by the Forest Service to show the assay certificates on these claims, Jerry stated that, along with considerable other personal belongings, these reports were lost several years ago in a fire, which destroyed a truck that housed them. The report also says Jerry is considered one of the best-informed and valued guides in the Mt. Baker/Boundary area. It states that Jerry may qualify for relief under Public Law 87-851. "The Mining Claim Occupancy Act." A mineral examination conducted by the Forest Service of Shuksan No. 1 indicated that no valuable deposits existed.

On Dec. 22, 1965, the Glacier District Ranger Kirkland wrote a letter to the forest supervisor in Bellingham recommending against contesting the claim. He recommended that the Forest Service issue to Jerry a special-use permit for his cabin. Kirkland stated that the reason he suggests this is that when Jerry goes to town, he gets drunk and becomes troublesome. Kirkland felt that, if left in the cabin, Jerry would be less a problem for the community and the county. Kirkland also stated that he was positive that if Jerry were put out of the cabin he would constantly be between jail and the welfare office.

Ranger Kirkland's viewpoint on the matter was not agreed with at the regional level. In May of 1966, he was directed again to compose another letter to Jerry to evict him from government land. In a memorandum in August by Kirkland to the Bellingham office, he informed them that Jerry has spent most of the summer in Silesia

Creek Drainage. The ranger was unable to contact him in regard to the eviction notice.

In 1967, there were at least three major hearings from the local level to the western region level dealing with the issue. All the hearings came up with the decision that Jerry must be moved now. Jerry on many occasions after getting liquored up paid a visit to the Glacier Ranger Station and set to tearing the place apart. One of the good boys with plenty of patience would then give him another free ride home. In the regional office hearing, 22 copies of Jerry's eviction notice were sent to different offices. At this time Jerry had the whole U.S. Forest Service buffaloed and scared to death of him.

On Jan. 5, 1970, the Bellingham office issued a letter dealing with the last three men who had residences in the Mt. Baker National Forest. Two of the three lived in the Glacier Ranger District. Ray Block lived on the Silver Tip Claim and the other was Jerry Bourn. At the request of the Forest Service, Ray Block agreed to move off his claim and the Forest Service burned his structures to the ground.

In this letter, it states that "Jerry did not respond to the latest letter. He can be difficult to approach and talk to because of drinking habits, which frequently leaves him belligerent. We feel we have to take stronger action to evict him as he usually has several large dogs near him and he frequently carries a rifle." The ranger added, "The last time I saw him, I asked him about resolving his occupancy problem. Jerry was drunk and we made no headway."

In the summer of 1975, Jerry submitted to the Forest Service a proposal to do mining work on his claim in the streambed of Silesia Creek, upstream a half-mile from where the creek enters Canada. The proposal was a well-conceived and documented plan in written form. The work involved placing a D7 bulldozer in the creek and moving the gravel over to a mechanical sluice box.

Employees of the Forest Service and Washington Game Department visited the site with Jerry and discussed the project. After a period of review, a government geologist was sent to determine if there was any minimal value at the site. He found none and the permit was turned down. It appeared from all the information in the archives that the government gave the application a fair review.

Another incident involving Jerry and the making of a footbridge across the Nooksack River caused deep distress with the Forest Service. Jerry was employed by an area logger who was logging a timber sale almost directly across the river from Jerry's cabin. Without a car or driver's license (however, that would not have made any difference), Jerry was forced to walk to work. To shorten the 15-minute commute, he decided to cut down a big beautiful fir tree to make a footbridge. After Jerry cut down the tree and removed the required limbs, it became a suitable footbridge. The Forest Service took about one week to investigate the down tree and headed to Jerry, accusing him of the act. Jerry reported that he had nothing to do with the act and felt that the wind must have blown it down. The Forest Service angrily told him that the tree had been cut by a chain saw and that someone wearing caulk boots was crossing on it. Jerry responded that he did not own a chain saw but admitted that he had been using it as a footbridge. It sure was handy, he added, but he sure did not know who cut the tree down. The Forest Service personnel again went away shaking their heads in disgust.

For seasons Jerry had been looking over this beautiful old-growth cedar tree, five feet in diameter, that was on his mining claim. With the high current price for cedar, he decided the time was right to cut it down and sell the cedar to a local shake mill.

After cutting it down, the Forest Service again came calling. They now told him it was not located on his claim but on Forest Service land. One thing led to another. The Forest Service filed a charge through Whatcom County on Jerry and he was sentenced to six months in the county jail.

When Jerry returned, the tree was lying where it fell. However, in a short period of time, the Forest Service placed the tree up for sale. The tree laid in complete view of Jerry's cabin.

When a possible bidder inspected the project, Jerry would go out to have a friendly discussion concerning the tree. Jerry repeatedly told each of the bidders that in his eyes, after spending six months in jail, he had paid the debt and now he was the legal owner of the tree. On the day of the sale, there was no bidder, and that tree is still in the same spot.

Bourn Tire Chain Business

When the Washington Highway Department enforced a law requiring chains be installed on vehicles traveling on to the Mt. Baker Ski area, Jerry operated, for about six to seven years, a business to provide these chains. This business required an old, well-used van truck with tire chains hanging on racks mounted to the outside walls. Inside the van were extra chains, repair kits, and jacks. This van would be parked at a wide spot in the highway and located at the point where chains were posted and required.

Jerry employed one or two high school students to perform the bulk of the work while he'd be having a drink or two from some friendly Canadian skier. The skiers had the chains installed, paid for the use of the chains, and left a deposit for returning the chains. In many cases, the deposit was greater than the value of the chains. Jerry always had a supply of wine in his van to help keep his body warm and in some cases he would leave early, keeping the deposit.

One day a Canadian did not have enough money for the deposit so he left his watch. After the man headed up the hill, Jerry took a real liking to the gold plated watch. The more wine he drank, the better he thought the watch looked on his wrist.

Later in the day with the watch then hidden away, the skier returned for chain removal and his deposit returned. After removing the chains, Jerry returned from the deposit box with the normal amount of cash. The skier said, "No, I demand my watch be returned." Jerry said, "No, you gave me money." A major argument followed for 10 minutes with Jerry repeatedly stating that there was no watch. Finally Jerry caved in and threw it at him, and yelled to him. "Don't come skiing up on my mountain again."

A Volkswagen car requiring chains had a serious problem of clearance for the chain to travel in the area of the wheel well. Jerry invented a chain link that he named the J Hook (J for Jerry). With periodical improvements being made to the hook over one winter and with the help of his sister, Jerry applied for a patent.

Jerry did not have sufficient funds for the patent, so next he notified the Campbell Chain Co. concerning his idea; however, the chain company did not respond. Within a few years, Campbell Chain added a new item to its product line, a J Hook that was similar to Jerry's J Hook.

The life of the chain van came to an end with Jerry driving off the road late one night a mile or two west of Maple Falls. The van plowed off the road, out into the trees, and stopped against a large tree. Jerry climbed out unhurt. While he was reviewing the damage in the darkness, the van exploded in fire and burned.

Jerry sadly stood back scrutinizing it until the fire burned out because it was late at night, no others were utilizing the road, and he was getting cold standing in the rain. The fire went out, so Jerry decided to crawl under the warm van and anticipate the arrival of the dawn.

Later in the early morning, a motorist reported the accident to the Sheriff's office. When two officers responded to the accident, they observed a man's legs sticking out from the burned-out van. As they were discussing how to go about the removal of the corpse of the burned victim, Jerry crawled out from the van, and said, "Well, it's about time you got here. A guy could have froze to death."

Bourn Hotel

Jerry was constantly in trouble with the different law agencies in Whatcom County. Some people in Glacier referred to the Whatcom County Jail as the Bourn Hotel. After spending a few months in jail, Jerry once called his sister Charlotte to inform her that he'd be released from the Whatcom County Jail tomorrow. Upon being released, he would call as she was standing by to drive him back to Shuksan.

As planned, Jerry did call, but this call was to inform her that he was now in the Bellingham jail. The moment he walked out of the county jail, the Bellingham Police were there with a warrant for a stay in the Bellingham jail.

In the Whatcom County jail, Jerry was popular and trusted by the guards. Each morning he'd be the first up to make the coffee, followed by starting the breakfast for all the inmates. He felt that going to jail in the winter was much nicer than being cabin-bound in the 10 feet of snow at his cabin, but the feeding of the animals was the problem.

From Feb. 27, 1956 to Dec. 19, 1974, Jerry was arrested 15 times by the Whatcom County Sheriff's Office on charges that included drunken driving, no drivers license, no vehicle insurance, assault, disorderly vagrant, destruction of property, and injury to state property. Jerry served in Whatcom County Jail a total of 555 days for these offenses.

The Washington State Highway Camp at Shuksan employed Jerry for one or two winters to perform all types of work from running snowplows to sweeping the floors. One long winter day at the cabin when he was not working and after a bottle of wine, he strolled the half-mile over the snow to the kitchen of the Highway Camp. Politely, he asked the cook who was preparing the evening meal to drive him to Glacier for added bottles of wine. Shortly afterward, an argument erupted as the cook stated that he was in the middle of cooking the evening dinner for the crew and could not possibly leave.

Jerry shook his head, stomped back to the cabin and got his 30-30 rifle, stomped back, and at gunpoint forced the cook to drive him to Glacier. Jerry obviously was fired by the state and had another visit from the Sheriff's Office, who removed all of Jerry's guns. Jerry hitched a ride as soon as possible to his longtime friend Jake Steiner and borrowed a rifle for hunting.

Jerry, Nell, and Jake drove to the monthly winter evening dance at the Dam Town Community Hall and at closing time the three headed home upriver. With Jake driving in the snow, Jerry ordered him to pull over on the Nooksack River Bridge beyond Glacier. Jerry and Nell climbed out of the truck and immediately were engaged in a fistfight. Jerry pulled off her shoes and threw them in the river.

After returning to Jerry's cabin, the three were having an early morning breakfast with all the anger of the past night forgotten. This year the Highway Department had plowed the snow to Jerry's driveway and beyond. After daylight, an automobile drove by at a slow speed, which created a barking frenzy from all eight dogs. Jerry made the statement that those guys were obviously staking out his place.

The automobile turned around up the road, returned slowly and parked in his driveway. When a stranger parked in his yard, Jerry normally

Red Lead claim shelter on Silesia Creek. (G. Byeman)

The shelter was the open-air type. (G. Byeman)

The shelter was made from available cedar materials. (G. Byeman)

Jerry down in the Red Lead with help. (G. Byeman)

Jerry taking the high route out above the Red Lead. (G. Byeman)

Hand panned gold from hand crushed ore. (R. Kramer)

Placing gold in glass jar. (R. Kramer)

Gold ready to be placed in hiding place. (R. Kramer)

shouted out, "Don't move an inch. I got you covered." On this occasion, the early morning visitors angered Jerry quickly, owing to the fact of his big hangover. He removed the rifle from the nails on the wall, and opened the door a crack. Now the car was an old Plymouth with a large winged hood ornament. Jerry quickly took aim and shot off the ornament. The car then fled in a great haste but the Sheriff returned in a couple of hours.

Canadian Air Disaster

On Dec. 9, 1956, the worst Canadian air disaster occurred when a TCA North Star crashed into Slesse Mountain just north of the U.S./Canada border. The iced-up plane could not maintain elevation and struck the mountain 100 feet from the top on the east side, killing all 62 people aboard. The crash occurred during a major winter storm. After striking the sheer face, the wreckage plunged down the 2,000-foot vertical face into the valley below.

The human remains were located without any valuables the following summer. Stories circulated of some wealthy foreign visitors traveling with large sums of money and jewelry. The RCMP made contact with the FBI and requested the opportunity to have a conversation with Jerry Bourn. The facts of that discussion were never made public, but there were surely questions asked. The RCMP asked if he had seen any strangers in the area of his mining claim, which is located at the point where Silesia Creek dumps into Canada. The FBI may

have asked Jerry if he had been to the site, but again that history is lost.

No other person including the Forest Service personnel matched Jerry's knowledge of the mountains in the Mt. Baker Ranger Station District. The Anderson, Swamp, Ruth, and Silesia Creek drainages were the main areas he felt held the promise of gold.

Red Lead

Jerry's main focus in his search for gold was in the Silesia Creek drainage either in the United States or in Canada. Many others did not care that the two were in separate countries. The most worked and recognized claim of Jerry's was the one which he titled the "Red Lead." The location of the Lead was on the steep hillside between the Red Mountain Mine and Silesia Creek. The Lead was made up of a large eroded rock basin and rock face above.

With this location somewhat in a line between the Jack, Gargett, and the Red, Jerry's knowledge assured him that being in line the Red Lead, when developed, would turn out equally rich. Jerry calculated that the water which ran off the surface of the Lead, if it could be traced, would show a rich gold deposit. Jerry placed some type of dye in the stream but could not pick up the dye downstream.

The Red Lead Camp was constructed at the bottom of the basin and Jerry erected three or four lean-to structures with all the roofs connected. The structures were made mainly from cedar and were built into the side of huge standing trees, mainly to shed water. Many items at the camp were from the Red Mountain Mine, which his brother owned. Items such as the cooking stove and beds were brought down.

Jerry performed a large amount of work on the rock face and in many cases Jerry rappelled by telephone wire down the face from the top. This basin and rock face were subject to many spring and early summer avalanches.

Also at this location, Jerry could keep an eye on his brother's mine and help himself to reworking the Red's tailing pile. Years were spent working this claim and he created some things that were unbelievable. One was an 80-foot bridge with railing across Silesia Creek and the other was a bathtub in the Silesia Creek bed. Jerry discovered a big, hollowed-out and rounded rock that was above the normal water line. Jerry took a star drill with a hammer, drilled a hole near the bottom and with short hose and a cork he created a natural bathtub.

In the early 1950's, the East Fork of Silesia Creek at Rapid Creek was the site of a massive forest fire that burned almost one whole summer. This fire was named the Rapid Creek Fire and a huge collection of firefighters was needed along with supplies. Because of the location in a remote area, a trail had to be built further up the East Fork of Silesia Creek.

The year after the fire, Jerry located another mining claim on Silesia Creek in the area of Rapid Creek. Jerry built a first rate enclosed cabin similar to the Shuksan Cabin at this new location. The furnishings were mostly items left over from the Rapid Creek Fire. Very little information is available concerning the Rapid Creek Claim and cabin.

Throughout the summers that Jerry spent on the two Silesia Creek claims, each year he repeatedly became acquainted with the Forest Service summer trail crew and knowledgeable of the location of that crew. Jerry and crewmembers encountered each other on the trails, and visited the other's camps.

Jerry, in the middle of the day, traveled into their camp while the crew was performing trail work and borrowed canned food. Jerry, being a smart thief, only took items that the Forest Service had a large quantity of, assuming that they would not miss a few cans. The missing cans became a season-long contest between the crew and Jerry, the thief. At different times, the crew foreman would station a man hidden near the camp for the day to keep an eye open for Jerry, but on these days he never came visiting.

One late afternoon, two Forest Service men decided to visit Jerry's camp and check out the cans. As they walked in, Jerry was preparing dinner. They looked at items on his shelves and saw peaches in the extra-large can of the same brand as in their camp.

Jerry after a hard day. (T. Brown)

Jerry detected their looks, took one of the cans, opened it, and offered them some. He told them that he purchased peaches at a wholesale store in Bellingham, and really likes the big cans because he'd sit down and eat the whole thing. They left walking back to their camp, shaking their head, and knew that he had them again.

Death of the Last Sourdough

On April 14, 1980 at about 2 a.m. Jerry Bourn was killed in a car wreck. He was a passenger in a friend's car who volunteered to drive him home following a long party night in Glacier. The accident occurred midway between Glacier and the cabin over the top of Power Plant Hill.

Jerry and cabin by candlelight. (G. Byeman)

Upon receiving word of his death, the Forest Service the following morning placed a lock on the cabin door and a sign that read "Property of the U.S. Government" was placed on the side of the cabin as the Forest Service did not want another Jerry. Jerry had won all the battles, but in the end the U.S. Government out-lasted him and won the war.

As word of Jerry's death spread within an hour throughout Glacier, vandals were at the cabin, broke in, and searched the cabin for the stash of gold that everyone knew he had. The vandals removed parts of the floor, went all though Jerry's personal items, and went as far as removing the chinking between the logs, thinking that the hidden gold was in the moss-type material.

Jerry made a game of creating booby traps in the cabin for anyone such as these vandals who broke in. One trap was a sealed can, which was attached to a ceiling joist in the corner of the second floor. The can had a lid that opened downward. When the lid was pried off, all his used razor blades came falling down on the thief. Another was a similar can nailed again on a high point on a joist. When one climbed up and reached in, one's hand found a large rat trap.

A Prince Albert Tobacco can was used for Jerry's gold storage. Lady, being accustomed to the vandals, allowed their passage. All the dogs and Tony, the horse, were adopted by local Glacier people. Jerry's treasured guestbook disappeared that day.

Chapter 9
Jack's Ghosts

The Lone Jack's first mill site is quiet except for the wind blowing through the large fir and hemlock trees with the sound of Silesia Creek cascading down in the creek bottom. The roar of the stamp mills and crusher with men shouting to be heard has now been absent for 100 years.

There is very little evidence that there had been so much activity in the past other than the level building site and the flume waterway leading to the south. The building site and the mile-long flume were dug by hand labor.

The other reminders were items remaining from some form of steel or cast iron. The stamp mills are lying on their sides. They had been moved aside so the whole footprint of the mill could be sluiced of gold that may have dropped and fallen though the cracks in the floor. The stamp mills, a crusher, gold separation pan, tramway cable and the sawmill are the only remnants of the equipment that remain except for items used in the cookhouse, such as a stove and washing basin.

The sole remaining building was not located only a level building site with a stove, bedsprings, and glass. With the fire and requirement of logging the millsite, the total area was cleared of all vegetation. But today, 100 years later, the area is covered once again in dense second-growth timber.

On the century-old trail directly below the Lone Jack vein, the trail switchbacks past a huge boulder sitting beside the trail. As one approaches this boulder, a large whistler (marmot) standing on the boulder lets out a high-pitched shrill call that gives warning to his family members and all other living things within a mile of the site. How many generations of whistlers have lived under this car-sized boulder and have these whistlers re-told the stories of the Lone Jack correctly?

Further up the steep side of Bear Mountain at the mine site, there is also no evidence of the operation that had created all that activity for 10 years. All the buildings and wood items are completely gone with only a few metal items to be found. The only visible items are the two adit entries and waste rock on the hillside below.

Inside the adit of the Lone Jack vein, there is also no evidence of man's creation except for the adits, drifts, and stope area, which will remain for hundreds of years. In the area where the upper tramway headwork structure was located, two flat areas carved from a steep rock face will remain visible for years to come along with the trail up through the meadows. The remnants of a tramway tower can be located near the top of the cliff edge.

Jack Post died on the Oregon Coast a lone broken man as stated earlier. Russ Lambert continued to practice law and lived until his death in Sumas. Lambert left a family of children, grandchildren, and great-grandchildren to Whatcom County, one being named Russ Lambert in his memory. Luman Van Valkenburg, as Lambert, lived the remainder of his life in Whatcom County and in turn left a full family tree.

Andrew ("Big Andy") Ecklund died while working at his farm near Marietta, north of Bellingham. In unloading lumber from the back of his pickup truck, he accidentally fell off the truck tailgate, striking his head in the fall. His twin granddaughters were the first to discover the accident. With all the dangers that Andy had lived through from travel on the high seas, the work at Blue Canyon Coal Mine, and then the Lone Jack, it seems ironic that an insignificant accident would cause the death of such a mountain of a man.

What happened and who was the four-year old boy that Big Andy carried into the mill? Oh, the stories he and his mother could have told of their life at the Jack. The Cress brothers and Moline all traveled to work at the Jack as teenagers and returned as men. Dave and John Cress settled on adjoining farms on the Y Road in Whatcom County with Moline settling nearby.

All of the major owners and shareholders of the Lone Jack other than those of Whatcom County are lost to history.

The Boundary Gold operation left no future history and the two partners do not resurface in further mining or Whatcom County history. There are only two pictures of the Boundary Gold Co. mine/mill site. One was received directly from Jack Post's granddaughter on Lopez Island and the picture was labeled the Lone Jack Mill.

Andy Ecklund with granddaughters. (A. Knapp)

What could have become of the Italian fellow named Tony Copan who committed the murder in the Lulu while working in 1916? Did he escape back to Italy and live like a king, or did he go back to use the Lone Jack gold money to feed a large family which may at the time have been suffering from some type of famine?

The largest failure in all of the Lone Jack history is that of the Brooks-Willis operation. Phillip Brooks died following the failure of this operation. Could this failure in any way have affected his life? Carl Willis apparently toiled for many years on the project and had expectations of a great return. If this operation had not been affected by the war and a major engineering error in the placement of the mill, could it have turned out to be a major producer of Northwest gold?

On Feb. 6, 2007, the dilapidated remains of the Charlie Anderson/Jerry Bourn cabin burned to the ground. Since this occurred during the snowboard championship races at the Mt. Baker Ski area, all investigation indicated that some young vandals caused the fire. But, maybe, could the fire have been lit by the ghosts of Charlie or Jerry after these years of neglect to their cabin that we, the current owners, have allowed?

So what is to show for all the effort of money, labor, and equipment at the Lone Jack? The Mt. Baker Mining Co. operation created a small return to the stockholders through the dividends paid and the sale to Brooks-Willis in 1925 but how much may have been funneled off before getting to the hands of the stockholders?

By federal law, all the gold of the Jack was required to be sold to the U.S. Mint. However, similar to other mining operations, some of the gold was sold on the black market in the United States and Canada.

In 1997, to celebrate the 100-year centennial of the Lone Jack, a centennial coin was minted in gold and silver versions and sold throughout Whatcom County. (See page 2)

One item survived, a gold heart-shaped locket presented from "Big Andy" Andrew Ecklund to his daughter Olga Pattison of Bellingham. Pattison gave the locket to the Whatcom Museum before her death. This locket can be viewed at the museum in Bellingham.

Olga Pattison locket.
(Whatcom Museum)

Index

A

Anderson Cabin, 153, 158
Anderson, Charlie, 149, 150, 154, 158, 177
Anderson, Tom,136, 138
Austin Pass, 23
Austin, Banning, 23

B

B.B. & B.C. Railroad, 14, 23, 25, 31, 34, 35, 40, 51, 53, 56, 62, 84
Bald Eagle, 55
Barber Camp, 27
Bear Mountain, 6, 15, 23, 41, 60, 62, 64, 70, 78, 99, 100, 104, 105, 119, 124, 134, 135, 136, 175
Bell, Lowella, 146
Bernard, C.F., 37
Birdwell, Matt, 29, 49
Bishop, J.C., 148
Blue Mountain Coal Mine, 83
Bodega Saloon, 14
Both, C.W., 151
Bottiger, Frank, 99
Boundary Gold Co., 97, 98, 99, 100, 101, 102, 176
Boundary Red Mine, 35, 36, 52, 116, 150, 151, 152
Bourn, Charlie, 106, 126, 134, 144, 145, 147, 148, 149, 151
Bourn, Charlotte, 146, 149, 151, 157, 168
Bourn, Jerry, 134, 143, 144, 146, 147, 149, 150, 152, 153, 154, 155, 156, 157, 158, 159, 160, 161, 162, 163, 164, 165, 166, 167, 168, 169, 172, 173, 174, 177
Bourn, Margaret, 144, 145, 146
Bourn, Tom, 150, 151, 152, 153, 155
Braithwaite, Tom, 151
Brooks, Josephine, 101, 102, 124, 125, 132, 136

Brooks, Phillip, 101, 102, 103, 116, 125, 126, 177
Brooks-Willis Metals, Inc., 102, 119, 124, 126, 132, 133, 177
Brown, Tom, 162
Broyles, Judge John, 27, 28, 89
Bullene, Harry, 124, 132, 134, 135, 155, 156
Bullene, John, 135, 136, 155, 156
Bullene, Mamie, 132, 135

C

Calkins, Richard, 136
Cascade Mountains, 5, 22, 23, 24, 51, 78, 97, 134, 135
Cascade State Wagon Road, 24, 25, 29
Chilliwack Lake, 30
Chilliwack River, 17, 30, 35, 44, 150
Clark, S.Q., 97, 98, 101
Cole, Robert,132, 133, 135, 136
Collender, S.A., 135, 138, 139
Connors, W.J., 49, 50, 51, 54
Copan, Tony, 99, 177
Cornell's Ranch, 26
Cress, David, 84, 85, 86, 87, 88, 176
Cress, John, 84, 85, 86, 87, 89, 96, 176
Crooks, Grover, 18, 19
Crossland, Francis, 116

D

Dahlmen, Gus, 100, 101
Dahlmen, Warner, 100, 101
Dalton, Clair, 142
Deadhorse Road, 26
Dick, Elaine, 135, 136
Diversified Development Co., 138, 139, 142
Dove, René, 163

E

E.Y. Grasett & Co., 37
Eaton, Lillian, 14
Ecklund, Andrew, 61, 68, 81, 82, 83, 84, 87, 88, 89, 90, 91, 92, 94, 95, 176, 177
English & Son, 47, 48, 49, 50, 53, 54, 83
Erickson, Dehardt, 143, 144
Excelsior Powerhouse, 34, 59, 152

F

Friede, Leo, 41, 44, 50, 81, 94, 100, 103

G

Garrison Brothers State Bank, 20
Garrison Creek, 63, 69, 77
Gilmore, Samuel, 61, 84, 85, 86, 87, 88, 89, 90
Glacier, 22, 34, 99, 104, 126, 142, 146, 148, 152, 153, 154, 156, 157, 162, 163, 165, 169, 174
Glacier Hotel, 146
Gold Hill, 26, 27, 28
Grant, A. Robert, 138
Great Excelsior Mine, 36, 37, 59

H

Hahn, Henry, 41, 42, 50, 53, 54, 62, 81, 86, 103
Hammond, I.B., 56, 57, 60, 61
Hammond Manufacturing Co., 56, 58, 61
Hannegan Pass, 23, 24, 27, 35
Helms, Niles, 100
Hinkle, Ben, 135, 136
Hipkope, 17, 85
Hogan, 15, 16

J

Jack, 62, 87, 88, 90, 94, 100, 106, 120, 142, 151, 155, 156, 172, 176
Jack's Fire, 94
Jennie, 47, 53
Jerry's Pond, 159

K

Keplinger, Clarence, 135, 136
Knuehmann, John, 11, 12

L

Lambert, Carrie, 21
Lambert, Russ, 5, 6, 8, 9, 11, 12, 13, 14, 15, 16, 17, 18, 19, 20, 21, 22, 30, 40, 41, 42, 43, 48, 49, 53, 54, 91, 95, 150, 176
Lewis and Clark Fair, 30
Lone Jack, 11, 12, 13, 15, 16, 21, 22, 25, 26, 27, 31, 35, 36, 37, 40, 41, 42, 43, 45, 46, 47, 48, 49, 50, 52, 53, 54, 55, 56, 59, 60, 61, 62, 63, 64, 68, 72, 79, 81, 82, 83, 84, 85, 86, 87, 88, 89, 90, 91, 92, 93, 94, 95, 96, 97, 99, 101, 103, 104, 105, 106, 116, 119, 124, 126, 132, 133, 134, 135, 136, 137, 138, 139, 147, 150, 151, 152, 155, 158, 159, 175, 176, 177
Lone Jack Claim, 11
Lone Jack Co., 136, 137, 138, 139
Lone Jack Resources, 138
Loop, Albert, 25
Loop's Inn, 25, 26, 47, 62
Lowry, Bert, 100, 150
Lulu, 45, 47, 49, 53, 55, 60, 82, 95, 100, 106, 134, 135, 138, 142, 177

M

Mamie Pass, 25, 26, 88
McClellan, John, 42
McKenzie's Livery Stable, 146
Moline, Olaf, 89, 90, 96, 176
Mount Baker Mining District, 22, 30, 31, 32, 33, 35, 37, 40, 41, 45, 48, 50, 52, 57, 61, 81, 90, 94 105, 135
Mt. Baker Development Co., 128, 146
Mt. Baker Gold Rush, 12, 23, 25
Mt. Baker Mining Co., 22, 42, 43, 44, 46, 47, 53, 54, 55, 56, 59, 62, 81, 84, 91, 92, 93, 94, 95, 97, 98, 100, 102, 103, 120, 177
Mt. Baker Mining District Rush, 29
Mt. Baker, 23, 24, 30, 81, 148, 153,
Mt. Shuksan, 23
Myers, Frank, 55

N

Nooksack Falls, 26, 29, 59
Nooksack Mining Co., 37, 38, 39
Nooksack River, 16, 23, 24, 25, 44, 48, 93, 99, 145, 149, 158, 159, 166, 169

Norton, W.H., 48

O

O'Brien, Betty, 153, 154
Orner, Martin, 99, 100

P

Pattison, Olga, 177
Pelton Water Wheel, 77
Peters, Bud 124
Post, Clifford,16, 17
Post, Jack, 5, 6, 8, 9, 11, 12, 13, 14, 15, 16, 17, 18, 20, 22, 40, 41, 42, 43, 48, 49, 53, 54, 55, 91, 95, 150, 176
Post-Lambert, 25, 47, 48, 50, 53, 54, 58, 61, 81, 92, 93, 94, 95
Post, Lillian, 16

R

Red Lead Mine, 161, 172
Red Mountain, 6, 30, 35, 52, 103, 105, 150, 151, 172
Ruth Creek Trail, 27
Ruth Creek, 11, 23, 25, 27, 35, 88, 172

S

Schow, Vern, 124
Secrist, Chris,139
Shuksan, 23, 27, 28, 46, 48, 49, 51, 57, 58, 60, 62, 83, 88, 89, 90, 104, 113, 143, 147, 152, 153, 154, 158, 163,
Sidney, 47, 53
Silesia Creek, 30, 44, 47, 63, 70, 92, 100, 105, 106, 120, 124, 135, 150, 161, 163, 165, 166, 172, 173, 175
Silver Tip Mine, 22, 35, 166
Slate Creek Mining District, 11
St. Marie, L.N., 55
Stanislawsky, Henry, 41, 43, 44, 46, 47, 50, 51, 53, 57, 58, 60, 83, 91
Steiner, Herman, 26, 145
Steiner, Jake, 169
Stone, Charles, 138, 139
Straka, Joe, 157
Sumas, 5, 11, 14, 15, 16, 17, 18, 19, 20, 21, 22, 23, 25, 30, 31, 38, 41, 42, 43, 50, 53, 57, 58, 62, 88, 95, 162, 176

Swail, Carrie, 20
Swamp Creek, 6, 26, 27, 43, 49, 50, 51, 52, 60, 62, 99, 119, 149, 172
Swinehart, J., 37

T

The Daily Reveille, 37, 60, 61
Thomas, George, 97, 98, 101
Thompson's Falls, 26
Trail City, 27, 28
Treutle, Jack, 5, 14, 28, 50, 53, 54, 55
Trimble, Harry, 41, 44
Twin Lakes Pass, 6, 59, 60, 62, 63, 88, 161
Twin Lakes, 5, 12, 15, 25, 27, 31, 37, 44, 45, 49, 60, 63, 83, 100, 119, 133, 135, 136, 139, 150, 163

U

U.S. Forest Reserve, 15, 20
Union City, 27
United States Land Monument No. 1, 47

V

Van Valkenburg, Luman, 5, 6, 9, 11, 12, 13, 21, 22, 40, 41, 42, 48, 53, 54, 91, 176
Van Valkenburg, Matilda, 22

W

Wells Creek, 26
Whatcom County Courthouse, 30, 39, 164
Whist, 47, 53, 138
Whist Creek, 6, 120
Wild Goose Pass, 23
Willis, Carl, 102, 103, 105, 106, 113, 116, 125, 126, 132, 177
Wilson Township, 27
Winchester 30/30, 15
Winchester Lake, 6
Winchester Mountain, 6, 15
Wm. N. Rath & Co., 37
Wright, C.C., 148

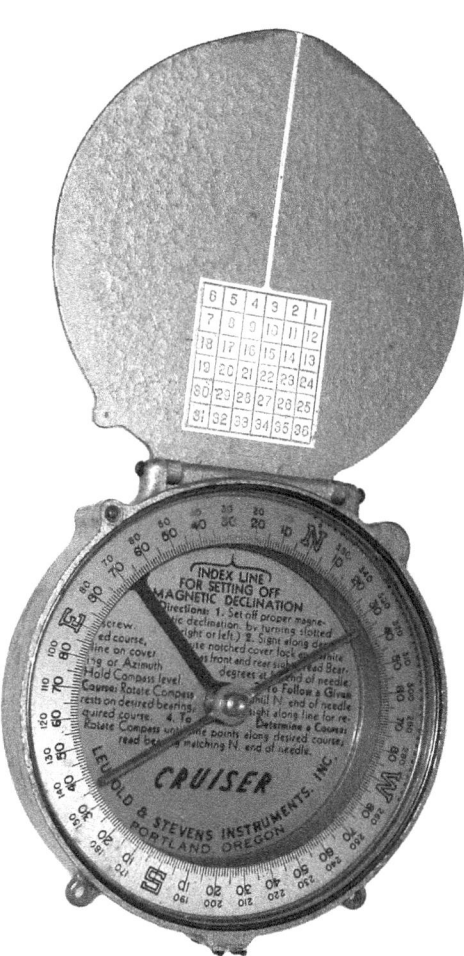

Map No. 1
*Anderson's map of
Mount Baker or Nooksack
Mining District*

Map No. 2
*General layout of surface
development at Lone Jack*

Map No. 3
*Lone Jack workings
1898 - 1907*

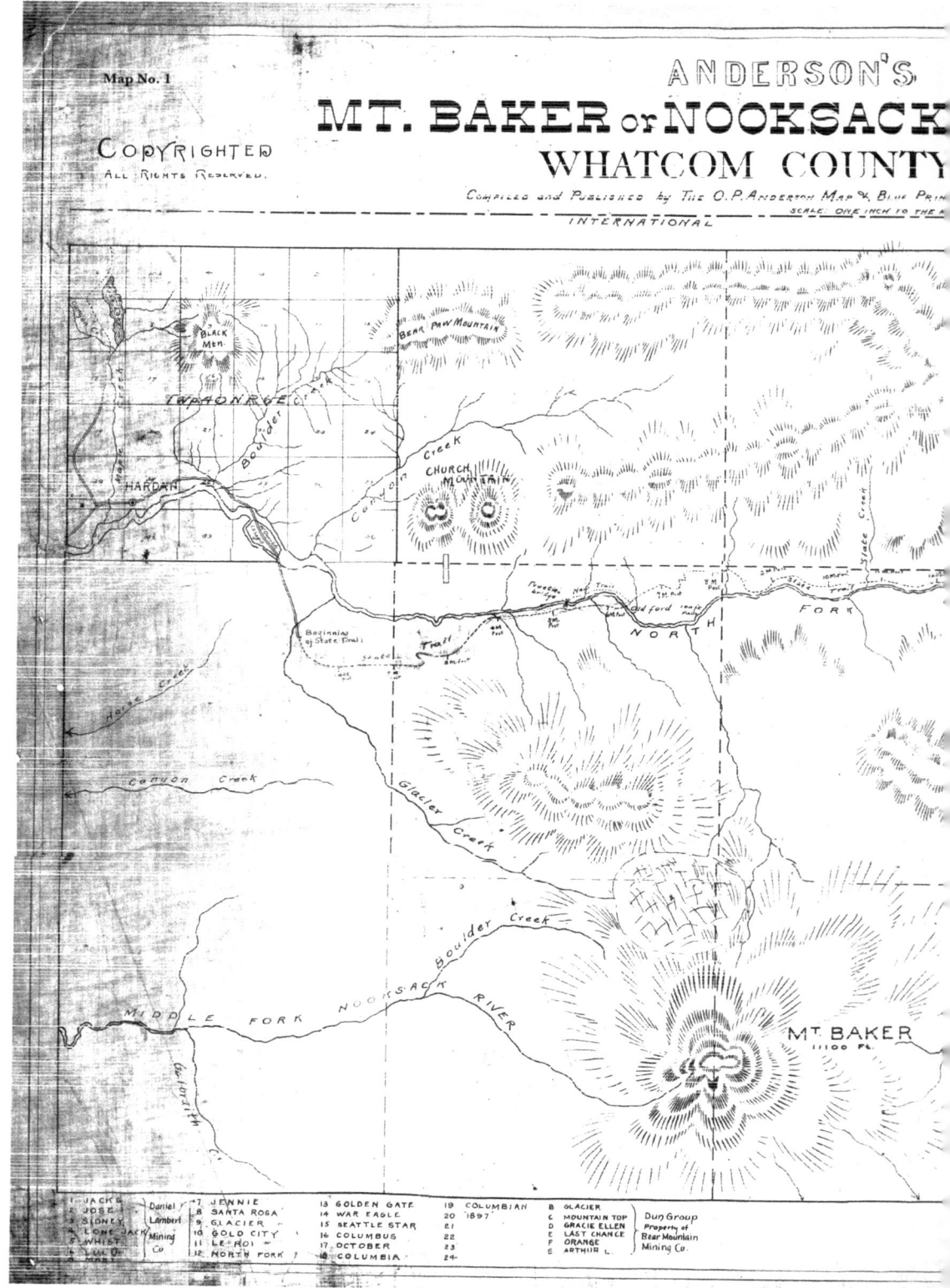

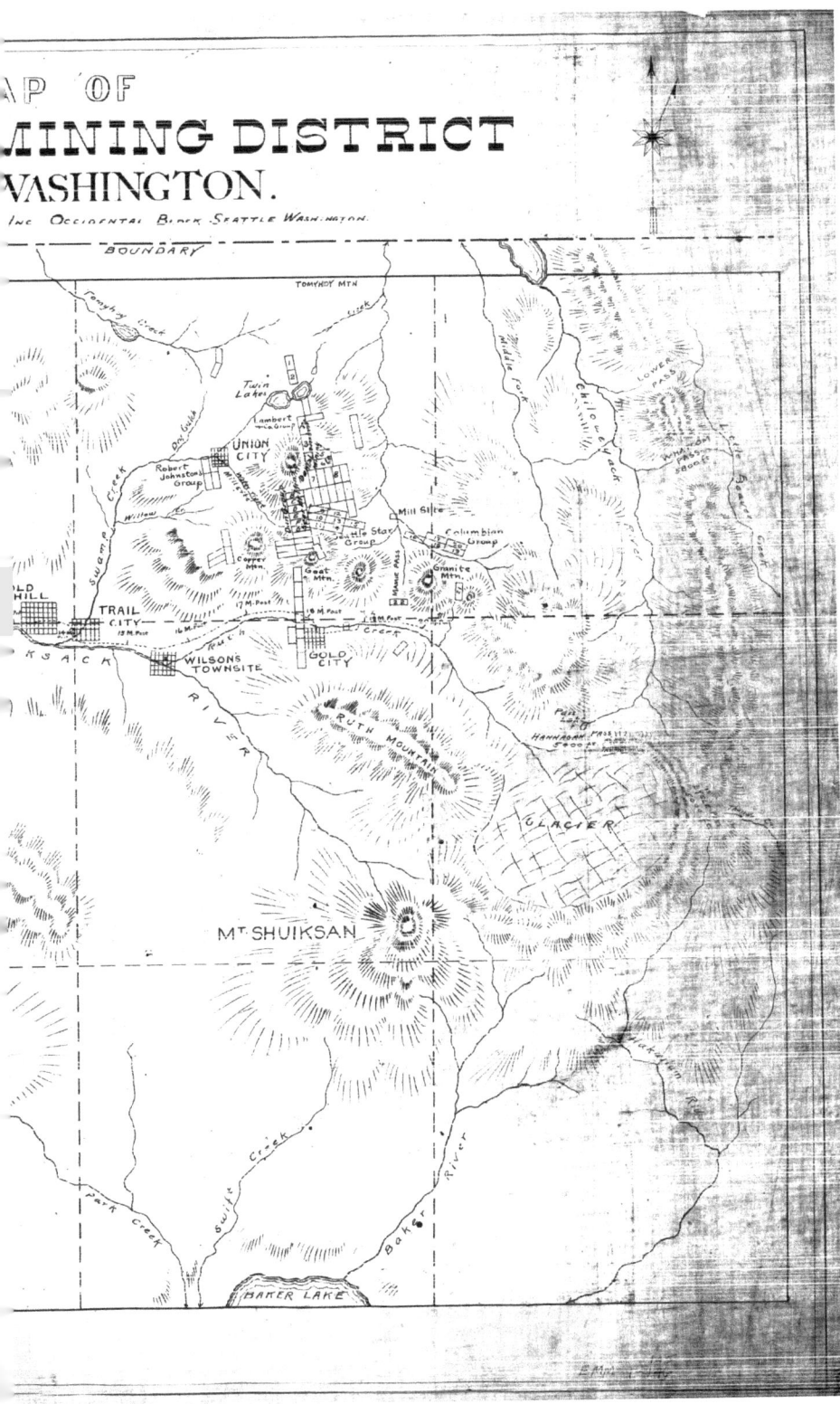

MAP OF
MINING DISTRICT
WASHINGTON.

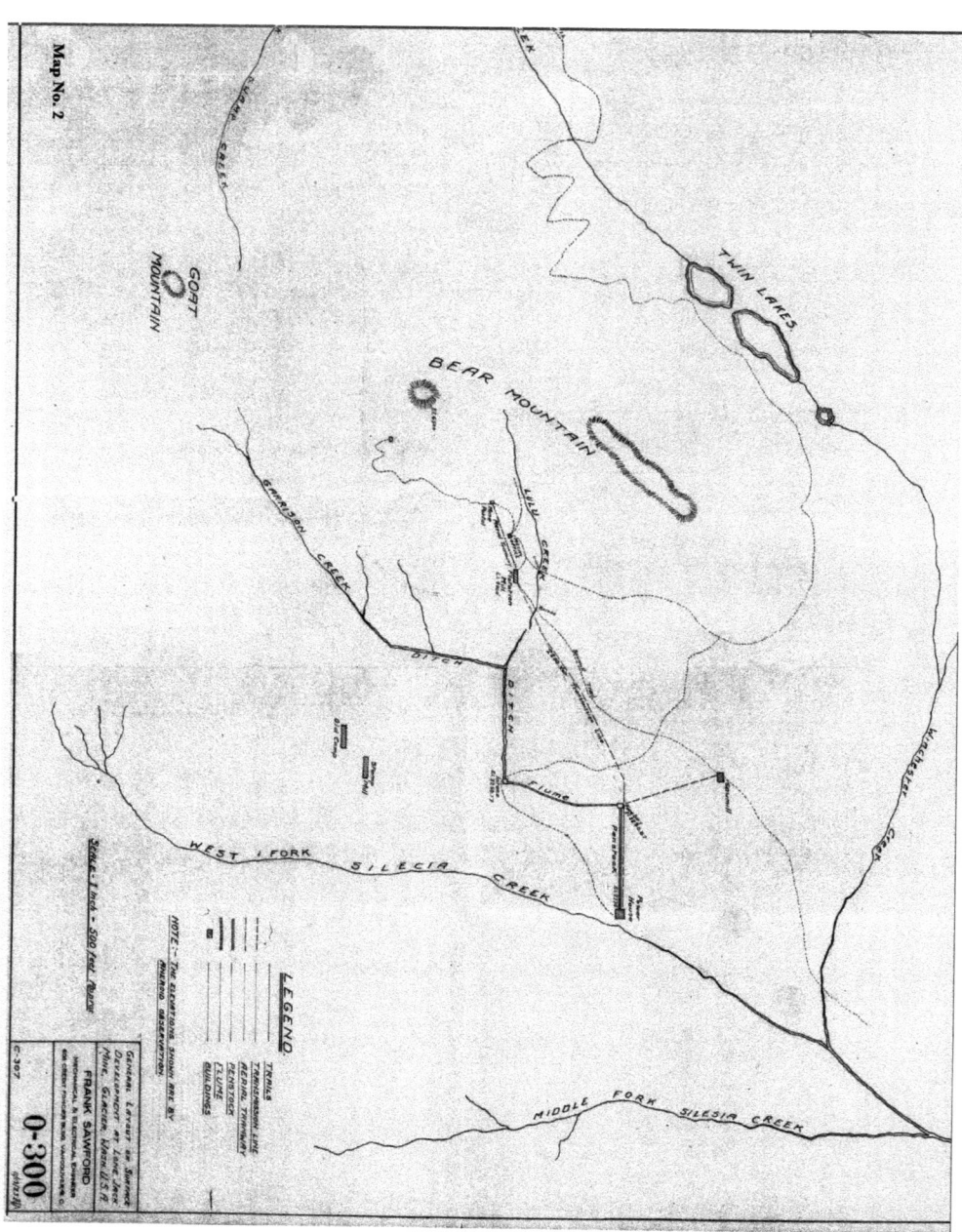

Map No. 2

GOAT MOUNTAIN

BEAR MOUNTAIN

TWIN LAKES

SAMPSON CREEK

LILY CREEK

DITCH

FLUME

WEST FORK SILECIA CREEK

MIDDLE FORK SILESIA CREEK

180

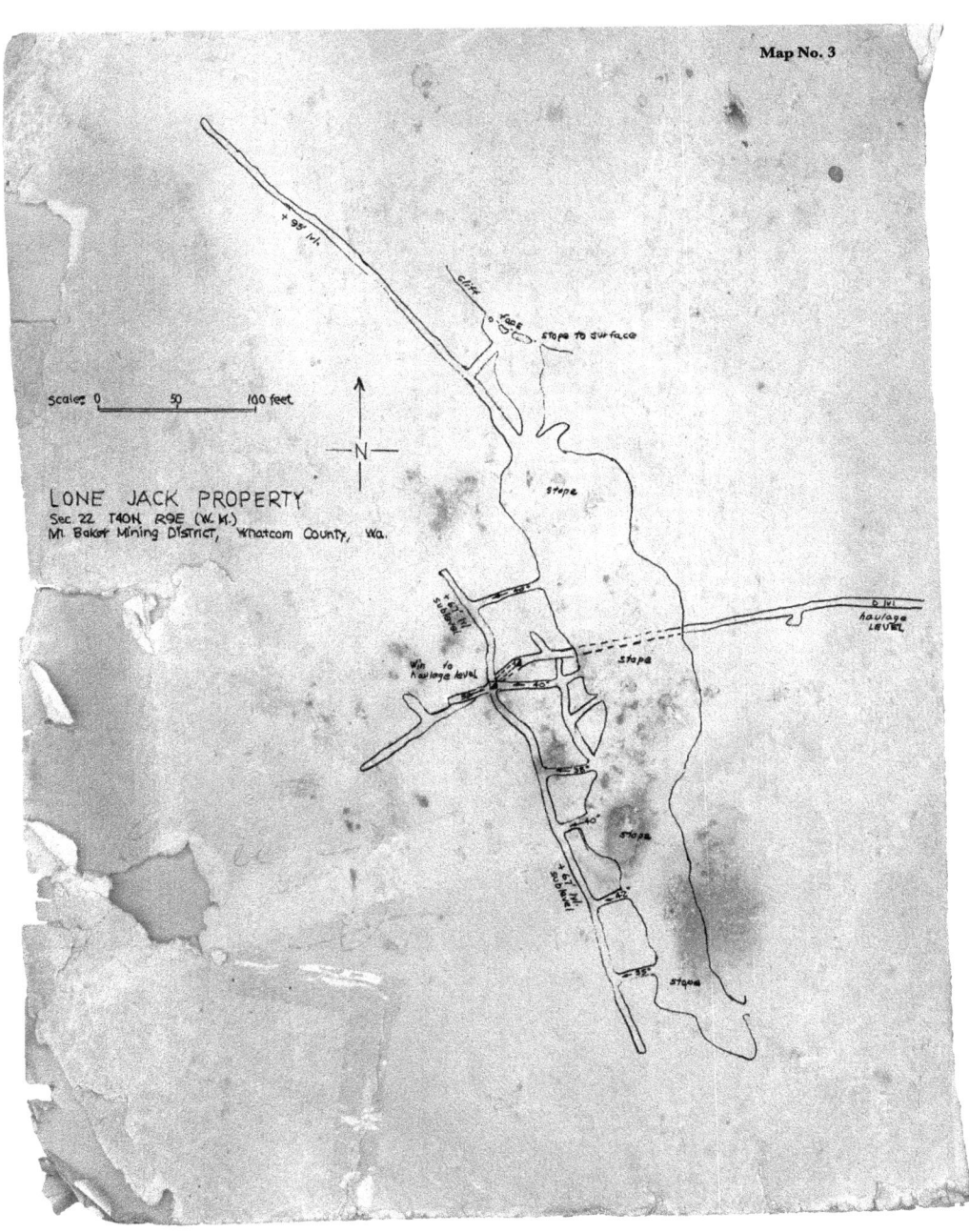

Scale: 0   50   100 feet

—N—

LONE JACK PROPERTY
Sec. 22 T40N R9E (W.M.)
Mt. Baker Mining District, Whatcom County, Wa.

stope to surface

stope

haulage LEVEL

stope

stope

stope

www.ingramcontent.com/pod-product-compliance
Lightning Source LLC
Chambersburg PA
CBHW041115120626
46547CB00019B/2713